Learn Spanish Blueprint For Beginners (2 in 1): Reach Intermediate Levels Fast With 50+ Complete Language Lessons- 1000+ Phrases& Words, Grammar, Short Stories& Conversations

Learn Intermediate Spanish In 30 Days: The Beginners Language Learning Accelerator- Short Stories, Common Phrases, Grammar, Conversations, Essential Travel Terms & Words In Context

TABLE OF CONTENTS

Introduction 1

I. Bases del español (Basics of Spanish) 3

    1. Pronombres personales / Personal Pronouns 3

    2. Artículos definidos e indefinidos / Definite and Indefinite Articles 4

    3. Géneros / Genders 4

    4. Estructuras singulares y plurales (Singular and plural estructures) 5

    5. Los adjetivos / The adjectives 5

    7. Partículas interrogativas 6

II. Los verbos en Español / The verbs in Spanish 7

    1. Verbos de primer grupo (First group verbs) 7

    2. Verbos de segundo grupo (Second group verbs) 7

    3. Verbos de tercer grupo (Third group verbs) 8

    4. Oraciones afirmativas, negativas e interrogativas – *Affirmative, Negative and Interrogative Sentences* 9

III. Los verbos irregulares / The irregular verbs 11

    1. Verbos ir / venir (Verbs "to go / to come") 11

    2. Verbos comunes irregulares 11

IV. La perífrasis verbal / Verbal Periphrasis 13

V. Verbos copulativos "ser y estar" / Copulative verbs "ser and estar" 14

    1. Verbo "ser" – Verb "ser" 14

    Verbo "estar" – Verb "estar" 14

    Vocabulario 15

    Vocabulario 15

VI. Verbos reflexivos / Reflexive verbs 17

    Verbos reflexivos de rutina diaria (Daily routine reflexive verbs) 17

    Verbos no reflexivos de rutina diaria (Non-reflexive daily routine verbs) 17

    Verbo quedar vs quedarse 18

    Verbo "parecer" vs "parecerse" 18

    Verbo encontrar vs encontrarse 19

    Verbo "ir" vs "irse" 19

VII. Adjetivos posesivos / Possessive Adjectives 21
Vocabulario 21
Vocabulario 22
Algunas nacionalidades (Some nationalities) 24

VIII. Preposiciones – Prepositions 26
Vocabulario 26
Vocabulario 29

IX. Los números y la fecha / The numbers and the date 31
1. Los números (Numbers) 31
2. Los días de la semana (The days of the week) 31
3. Meses del año 32

X. Adjetivos demostrativos / Demonstrative adjectives 34

XI. Verbo "Gustar" / Verb "to like" 36
Vocabulario 36
Vocabulario 37

XII. Comparaciones / Comparisons 39
Oraciones comparativas / Comparative sentences 39
Oraciones superlativas / Superlative sentences 39
Comparaciones de igualdad / *Comparisons of equality* 40

XIII. Adverbios / Adverbs 42
Adverbios de tiempo / Adverbs of time 42
Adverbios de frecuencia 42
Adverbios de lugar / *Adverbs of place* 43
Adverbios de modo / *Adverbs of manner* 43
Adverbios de aproximación 43

XIV. Tiempo presente continuo / Present continuous tense 46
Vocabulario 47

XV. Pronombres personales tónicos / Tonic personal pronouns 51

XVI. Tiempo Pasado Simple / Simple Past Tense. 57
Conjugación del verbo "-ar" / *Conjugation of the verb "-ar"* 57
Conjugación del verbo "-er" / *Conjugation of the verb "-er"* 57
Conjugación del verbo "-ir" / *Conjugation of the verb "-ir"* 58
Preguntas en Pasado Simple / *Simple Past Questions.* 58

Afirmación en Pasado Simple / *Simple past affirmation* 59

Negación en Pasado Simple / *Simple Past Negation* 59

Verbos irregulares en tiempo pasado simple / *Irregular verbs in simple past tense* 59

XVII. Preposiciones de lugar / Prepositions of place 63

XVIII. Pronombres Posesivos / Possessive Pronouns 70

Possessive pronouns 70

XIX. The possessive using "apostrophe « s »" in Spanish 71

XX. Los pronombres objeto directo 74

XXI. Pronombres objeto indirecto / Indirect Object Pronoun 78

XXII. Pronombre "Lo / La" vs Pronombre "Le" / Pronoun "Lo / La" vs Pronoun "Le" 81

XXIII. Religiones y doctrinas / Religions and doctrines. 83

XIV. Conectores / *Connectors.* 86

Conectores Aditivos / *Additive connectors.* 86

Conectores Adversarios / *Adversative connectors* 87

Conectores Consecutivos / *Consecutive connectors* 87

Conectores explicativos / *Explanatory Connectors* 88

Conectores concesivos / *Concessive connectors* 89

Conectores recapitulativos / *Recapitulatives Connectors* 89

Conectores de Ordenación / *Sort connectors* 89

XXV. Conjunciones / Conjunctions 91

XXVI. Verbos esenciales / Essential verbs 94

Para viajar / *For travelling* 94

En el restaurante / *In the restaurant* 94

Para trabajar / *For working* 95

Para cocinar / *For cooking* 96

Para conversar / *For talking* 96

Para festejar / *For partying* 97

CONCLUSION 98

Introduction

Hola and welcome to Learn Spanish in Your Car for Beginners. First, we would like to sincerely thank you and congratulate you for having made this amazing decision of investing on this incredible book that will help you learn the foundations of Spanish while you keep going through your daily routine, driving, walking or cooking!

As we know now, Spanish has become one of the most popular languages worldwide. This is directly translated as many people willing to connect to other cultures, companies wanting to explore new markets. Artists, businesspersons, tourists, culture and language lovers feel attracted by this beautiful, creative and poetic language that is now the third most spoken language. So, *felicitaciones* again for giving the first step towards what will become a tool to connect with new opportunities!

This book will become your best partner throughout your learning process. As we go, chapter by chapter, you will have the opportunity to understand the game rules of Spanish language, which will consolidate a steady base that will allow you to grow and build an entire structure full of grammar concepts, vocabulary, tips and many hours of listening practice.

Our system

This book was created to help you learn this amazing language in the simplest way and that's why we've decided to divide every topic into different chapters that will give you the idea of what you will start learning during your daily lesson.

Throughout these chapters, you will have the opportunity to start your learning process from the very basics of Spanish, which will not only make you repeat word after word and force your brain to try to understand why, but also it will include quick notes and a highly organized structure that will clear your doubts as you listen the vocabulary.

This book will be divided into 30 chapters. Every chapter will be titled with a specific topic, like "Pronouns", for example.

At some points during the chapters, you will have the opportunity to listen to short stories or dialogues that will help you go deep into the real use of Spanish in daily-life conversations.

Some of the chapters will also include specific vocabulary that will give you extra ideas about how Spanish works and how to combine the main topics with these new words you will learn.

For each and every word, it will first be presented in it's Spanish form and then the English form. Some of the subcategories will introduce only translations and some others will contain a sentence using that particular Spanish word into context.

For dialogues and stories, you will first listen to a longer paragraph in Spanish, and then you will have to opportunity to listen to its translation in English. This as part of your system to help you accelerate your learning process and take fully advantage of these amazing 10 hours of complete audio practice that will give you a great level in Spanish in 30 days.

Finally, some of the topics will include an introductory paragraph as well as quick notes and interesting facts that will not only allow you to learn new words by listening and repeating, but also to have a full understanding of this beautiful language.

Before we begin…

We want you to know that learning a new language can be challenging and confusing at times. At Excel Language Lessons, we are focused on providing the easiest, clearest and most concise guides for beginners to learn new languages. With that being said, it is up to you to apply yourself in order to achieve your bilingual goals and become an expert through the process of reading our proven guides.

We would like to thank and congratulate you on your decision to purchase this book; it takes a lot of courage and due diligence to take on a new language!

So let's get ready and prepare our minds to start this amazing journey throughout the romantic world of español!

¡Comencemos! Let's begin!

I. Bases del español (Basics of Spanish)

1. Pronombres personales / Personal Pronouns

Yo – I
Yo soy latino
I am latino

Tú – You (informal, singular)
Tú hablas español
You speak Spanish

Él – He
Él vive en México
He lives in México

Ella – She
Ella bebe café
She drinks coffee

Nosotros, Nosotras - We (masculine or neutral and feminine form respectively)
Nosotros tenemos una casa
We have a house

Usted – You (formal, singular)
Usted es profesor
You are a professor

Ustedes – You (plural)
Ustedes bailan salsa
You guys dance salsa

Ellos – They (masculine form)
Ellos trabajan mucho
They work a lot

Ellas – They (feminine form)
Ellas son actrices
They are actresses

2. Artículos definidos e indefinidos / Definite and Indefinite Articles

El – The (singular, masculine)
El perro
The dog

La – The (singular, feminine)
La casa
The house

Los – The (plural, masculine)
Los niños
The boys

Las – The (plural, feminine)
Las niñas
The girls

Un – A / An (singular, masculine)
Un perro
A dog

Una – A / An (singular, plural)
Una casa
A house

Unos – Some (masculine)
Unos perros
Some dogs

Unas – Some (feminine)
Unas niñas
Some girls

3. Géneros / Genders

Género masculino / Masculine gender
In Spanish, letter "o" at the end of a word, creates the masculine form of a noun or adjective.
Perro / Male dog
Niño / Boy
Apartamento / Appartment
Carro / Car
Género femenino / Feminine gender
In Spanish, letter "a" at the end of a word, creates the feminine form of a noun of adjective.

Perra / Female dog
Niña / Girl
Casa / House
Bicicleta / Bicycle
Following this rule, we can combine nouns with articles, matching gender and quantity.
El perro en el apartamento - The male dog in the appartment
Un niño en la casa - *A boy in the house*
La bicicleta de la niña - *The bicycle of the girl*

4. Estructuras singulares y plurales (Singular and plural estructures)

In Spanish, as in English, letter "s" defines the plural form of all nouns and adjectives (with some exceptions).
El niño; Los niños - *The boy ; the boys*
La casa: las casas - *The house; the houses*
Un carro; unos carros - *A car; some cars*
Una manzana; unas manzanas - *An Apple; some apples*

5. Los adjetivos / The adjectives

In Spanish, adjectives have to match two specific factors: gender and quantity.
Adjetivos masculinos / Masculine adjectives
El niño alto - *The tall boy*
Los niños altos - *The tall boys*
Un apartamento bonito - *A pretty appartment*
Unos apartamentos bonitos - *Some pretty appartments*
Adjetivos femininos / Feminine adjectives
La niña alta - *The tall girl*
Las niñas altas - *The tall girls*
Una casa bonita - *A pretty house*
Unas casas bonitas - *Some pretty houses*

Vocabulario (Adjetivos) – Vocabulary (adjectives)

a. Altura y peso (height and weight)

Alto / Alta – *Tall*
Pequeño / Pequeña – *Small or Short*
Flaco / Flaca – *Skinny*
Gordo / Gorda – *Fat*
Grande – Big (both masculine and feminine)

b. Colores (Colors)

Rojo / roja – *Red*
Amarillo / amarilla – *Yellow*
Azul – blue (both masculine and feminine)
Verde – green (both masculine and feminine)
Naranja – orange (both masculine and feminine)
Morado / morada – *purple*
Blanco / Blanca – *White*
Negro / Negra – *Black*

c. Apariencia (appearance)

Bonito / bonita – *Pretty*
Hermoso / hermosa – *Beautiful*
Feo / Fea – *Ugly*

7. Partículas interrogativas

¿Qué? – What?
¿Qué hora es?
What time is it?

¿Quién? – Who?
¿Quién quiere pizza?
Who wants pizza?

¿Cómo? – How?
¿Cómo estás?
How are you?

¿Cuándo? – When?
¿Cuándo vienes a la fiesta?
When are you coming to the party?

¿Por qué? – Why?
¿Por qué aprendes español?
Why do you learn Spanish?

¿Dónde? – Where?
¿Dónde vives?
Where do you live?

Fin del capítulo / *End of chapter*

II. Los verbos en Español / The verbs in Spanish

1. Verbos de primer grupo (First group verbs)

In Spanish, verbs change their structures when conjugated. All first group verbs end with syllable "ar" and all of them –with few exceptions- are considered "regular verbs" which means, they follow the same conjugation rule.

Conjugación de verbos de primer grupo / Conjugation of first group verbs
Verbo "hablar" – "To speak"
Yo hablo - I speak
Tú hablas - You speak
Él habla - He speaks
Ella habla - She speaks
Nosotros hablamos, nosotras hablamos - We speak
Usted habla - You speak
Ustedes hablan - You speak (plural)
Ellos hablan, ellas hablan - They speak

Practica de conversación – Diálogos (Conversation practice – Dialogues)
1) ¿Tú hablas español? – *Do you speak Spanish?*
Sí, yo hablo español. – *Yes, I speak Spanish.*

2) ¿Ella baila salsa? – *Does she dance salsa?*
No, ella no baila salsa. – *No, she doesn't dance salsa.*

3) ¿Ustedes pintan la casa hoy? – *Do you guys paint the house today?*
Sí, nosotros pintamos la casa hoy – *Yes, we paint the house today.*

4) ¿Juan trabaja en una oficina? – *Does Juan work in an office?*
No, Juan trabaja en un hotel – *No, Juan Works in a hotel.*

Fin del diálogo– *End of the diálogo*

2. Verbos de segundo grupo (Second group verbs)

In Spanish, second group verbs include irregular verbs, but some others follow the same rule always.
Verbo "comer" – "To eat"
Yo como - I eat
Tú comes - You eat
Él come - He eats

Ella come - She eats
Nosotros comemos, nosotras comemos - We eat
Usted come - You eat
Ustedes comen - You eat (plural)
Ellos comen, Ellas comen - They eat

Practica de conversación – Diálogos (Conversation practice – Dialogues)
1) ¿Tú comes burritos? – *Do you eat burritos?*
Sí, me encantan los burritos. – *Yes, I love burritos.*

2) ¿Comen con nosotros esta noche? – *Do you guys eat with us tonight?*
No, no podemos – No, we can't.

3) Los niños comen muchos dulces – *Kids eat a lot of candies*
Sí, lo sé – *Yes, I know.*

Fin del diálogo– *End of the diálogo*

---

3. Verbos de tercer grupo (Third group verbs)

In Spanish, third group verbs are considered irregular verbs, as they don't follow the same conjugation rule. However, you can find multiple third groups verbs that will have the same structure.

Verbo "vivir" – To live
Yo vivo - I live
Tú vives - You live
Él vive - He lives
Ella vive - She lives
Nosotros vivimos, Nosotras vivimos - We live
Usted vive - You live
Ustedes viven - You live (plural)
Ellos viven, Ellas viven - They live

Practica de conversación – Diálogos (Conversation practice – Dialogues)
1) ¿Dónde vives tú? – *Where do you live?*
Yo vivo en Cuba. – *I live in Cuba.*

2) ¿Maria vive con su mamá? – *Does Maria live with her mom?*
Sí, ella vive con su mamá – *Yes, she lives with her mom*

3) Sr. Rodriguez, ¿usted vive solo? – *Mr. Rodriguez, do you live alone?*
Sí, yo vivo solo. – *Yes, I live alone.*

Fin del diálogo– *End of the diálogo*

4. Oraciones afirmativas, negativas e interrogativas – *Affirmative, Negative and Interrogative Sentences*

Introduction: In English, according to the type of sentence and verbs, you need to add auxiliar words to answer, deny and create an interrogative structure. For example, "you eat an apple" has to have an additional verb when changing into a interrogative sentence, i.e. "do you eat an apple?"

However, these additions are not necessary in Spanish, not even the common switching when using verb "to be", for example: "you are a doctor" – "are you a doctor?"
Vamos a los ejemplos / Let's go to the examples.

Oraciones afirmativas versus oraciones negativas – Negative versus affirmative sentences

Yo vivo en Honduras – *I like in Honduras*
Yo no vivo en Honduras – *I don't live in Honduras*

Maria quiere café – *Maria wants coffee*
María no quiere café – *Maries doesn't want coffee*

Nosotros bailamos salsa – *We dance salsa*
Nosotros no bailamos salsa – *We don't dance salsa*

Tú estás cansado / *You are tired*
Tú no estás cansado / *You are not tired*

Oraciones interrogativas – Interrogative sentences

¿Quieres pizza? – *Do you want pizza?*
¿Tienes hijos? – *Do you have kids?*
¿Te gusta el español? – *Do you like Spanish?*
¿Estás en México? – *Are you in Mexico?*

Respuestas – *Answers*

Sí, sí me gusta la pizza – *Yes I do like pizza*
No, no me gusta la pizza – *No, I don't like pizza*

Sí, tengo 3 hijos – *Yes, I have 3 kids*
No, no tengo hijos – *No, I don't have kids*

Sí, estoy en México – *Yes, I'm in Mexico*

No, no estoy en México – *No, I'm not in Mexico.*

Quick note: As you can see, answers are simple and do not require any additional word rather than *"Sí"* or *"No"*. Actually, it is completely correct to answer only by saying *"Sí / no"* without using any other verb or something similar to "I do", "I have", "I don't", "I am"…
About negative sentences, you can see that, in Spanish, you only need to add the word "no" always *before* the verb, regardless the kind of verb you are using.

Fin del capítulo / *End of chapter*

III. Los verbos irregulares / The irregular verbs

1. Verbos ir / venir (Verbs "to go / to come")
Conjugación / Conjugation
Ir (to go)
Yo voy - I go
Tú vas - You go
Él va - He goes
Ella va - She goes
Nosotros vamos, Nosotras vamos – We go
Usted va - You go
Ustedes van – You (plural) go
Ellos van, Ellas van – They go

Verbo "venir" – Verb "to come"
Conjugación – Conjugation
Yo vengo – I come
Tú vienes – You come
Él viene – He comes
Ella viene – She comes
Nosotros venimos, Nosotras venimos – We coe
Usted viene – You come
Ustedes vienen – You (plural) come
Ellos vienen, Ellas vienen – They come

Pequeña historia – Short story
Juan va; Juan viene – Juan goes; Juan comes

Todos los días, Juan va a la universidad en bus – *Every day, Juan goes to the university by bus.*
Los fines de semana, Juan va a casa de su mamá – *On weekends, Juan goes to his mom's house.*
Usualmente, Juan va a casa de su mamá en taxi – *Usually, Juan goes to his mom's house by taxi.*
Juan, ¿cuándo vienes a la casa hoy? – *Juan, When do you come home today?*
Mamá, voy a las 8:00, como siempre – Mom, I go at 8:00, as always.

Fin de la historia – *End of the story*

---

2. Verbos comunes irregulares

Verbos "tener, querer, hacer, poder" – Verbs "to have, to want, to do, can / may"

Yo puedo hablar español - *I can speak Spanish*

María quiere un trabajo nuevo – *Maria wants a new job*

¿Qué haces esta noche? – *What do you do tonight?*

¿Cuántos años tienes? – *How old are you?*

Tengo 22 años – *I'm 22 years old*

Quick note: in Spanish, they literally say: "How many years do you have?"

¿Cuántos hijos tienen ellos? – *How many kids do they have?*
Hoy queremos ir a la playa – *Today we want to go to the beach*

¿Pueden venir a la fiesta esta noche? – *Can you guys come to the party tonight?*

Normalmente yo hago todo el trabajo – *Normally I do all the work*

Quiero aprender español – *I want to learn Spanish*

IV. La perífrasis verbal / Verbal Periphrasis

Introduction: as in English, a sentence can have more than two consecutive verbal structures either to create complex tenses such as "would have done" or simpler sequences like "have to do" or "can do". These combinations are called verbal periphrasis, but in Spanish, they don't work in the same way as in English.

In Spanish there are specific rules which you will learn in this book. But, for now, you can focus on the most basic of them: When you have two verbs together, in Spanish you will only conjugate the first one and leave the second action unconjugated.

Perífrasis con "Tener que" / Periphrasis with "Have to"

Tengo que comprar comida / *I have to buy food*
Tenemos que visitar a José / *We have to visit José*
Maria tiene que ir a la playa / *Maria has to go to the beach*

Perífrasis con "Querer" / Periphrasis with "Want to"

Quiero ir a Mexico este año / *I want to go to Mexico this year*
¿Quieres cenar conmigo? / *Do you want to have pizza for dinner?*
Queremos aprender español / *We want to learn Spanish*

Perífrasis con "Poder" / Periphrasis with "Can"

¿Puedes hablar español? / *Can you speak Spanish?*
¿Puedo ir contigo a la fiesta? / *Can I go with you to the party?*
Las aves pueden volar / *Birds can fly*

Perífrasis con "ir a" / Periphrasis with "Go to"

Vas a practicar en la biblioteca / *You go to practice in the library*
María va a hacer ejercicio / *Maria goes to do exercise*
Quick note 1: This specific periphrasis works as a future tense and can be translated as "going to" in English.
Quick note 2: The English structure "Let's" as in "Let's eat" has a similar version in Spanish and it's created by conjugated "ir" with pronoun "nosotros" or "nosotras". For example:

Vamos a comer / *Let's eat*
Vamos a practicar / *Let's practice*

Fin del capítulo / *End of chapter*

V. Verbos copulativos "ser y estar" / Copulative verbs "ser and estar"

Introduction: in Spanish, the actions of being someone or something and being somewhere are explained using a different verb. Situations such as identification, description and definition will be expressed using "ser".
On the other hand, from a general point of view, verb "estar" will describe location, feelings and emotions.
Both verbs "ser" and "estar" have the same translation in English: "to be" but they will be used in total different contexts and both are considered irregular verbs.

1. Verbo "ser" – Verb "ser"
Conjugación
Yo soy estudiante – *I am a student*
Tú eres bueno – *You are good*
Él es alto – *He is tall*
Ella es latina – *She is latina*
Nosotros somos argentinos – *We are Argentinians*
Usted es el señor Gonzales – *You are mister Gonzales*
Ustedes son amigos – *You guys are Friends*
Ellas son cristianas – *They are Christians*

Verbo "estar" – Verb "estar"
Conjugación
Yo estoy en Colombia – *I'm in Colombia*
Tú estás feliz – *You are happy*
Él está ocupado – *He is busy*
Ella está en la avenida Diego Fernandez – *She is in the Diego Fernandez Avenue*
Nosotros estamos cerca – *We are close*
Usted está cansado – *You are tired*
Ustedes están en México – *You guys are in Mexico*
Ellos están aquí en casa – *They are here at home.*

Pequeña historia – Short story

¿Dónde está Juan? – *Where's Juan?*
¿Dónde está tu hermano? – *Where's your brother?*
Él está en casa de Pedro – *He's at Pedro's house*
¿Quién es Pedro? – *Who's Pedro?*
Pedro es un amigo de la escuela – *Pedro is a friend from school*
Tengo que llamar a su casa, es muy tarde. Son las 10 pm. – *I have to call to his house, it's very late. It's 10 pm.*

<u>On the phone</u>**:** Hola Pedro ¿Cómo estás? – *Hi Pedro how are you?*
Estoy bien, gracias. – *I'm fine, thank you.*
¿Juan está en tu casa? – *Is Juan in your house?*
Sí, él está aquí. – *Yes, He is here*

Fin del diálogo – *End of the dialogue*

Vocabulario

<u>Profesiones I (Professions I)</u>

Quick note: In Spanish, most of the professions also have gender, which mean, a word like "lawyer" will have a masculine and a feminine form.

Abogado, Abogada / *Lawyer*
Maestro, Maestra / *Teacher*
Doctor, Doctora / *Doctor*
Ingeniero, Ingeniera / *Engineer*
Vendedor, Vendedora / *Seller*
Contador, Contadora / *Accountant*
Cocinero, Cocinera / *Cook*
Panadero, Panadera / *Baker*

Práctica conversación – Diálogos (Conversation practice – Dialogues)
1) ¿Cuál es tu profesión? - *What's your profession?*
Soy profesor de matemáticas - *I'm a math teacher*

2) Yo soy abogada, me gusta ayudar a otros – *I'm a lawyer, i like to help others*
¿Y te gusta tu profesión? – *And do you like your profession?*
Si, me encanta – *Yes, I love it*

3) Hoy voy a casa de un amigo, él es cocinero – *Today I go to to a friend's house, he is a cook.*
¿Puedo ir contigo? - *Can I go with you?*
Claro – *Of course*
Fin del diálogo– *End of the dialogue*

Vocabulario

<u>Emociones y sentimientos I (Emotions and feelings I)</u>

Feliz / *Happy*
Hoy estoy feliz / *I'm happy today*

Triste / *Sad*
María está triste y no sé por qué / *Maria is sad and I don't know why*

Molesto, Molesta / *Angry*
Los niños están molestos / *The kids are angry*

Cansado, Cansada / *Tired (masculine and femenine form)*
Juan está cansado. Tiene mucho trabajo / *Juan is tired. He has a lot of work*

Emocionado, Emocionada / *Excited (masculine and feminine form)*
¡Estoy muy emocionada por la fiesta! / *I'm very excited for the party!*

Quick note: there are feelings in Spanish that won't use the same verb "to be" as in English in situations like "I'm afraid" or "I'm hungry", on the contrary, in Spanish, feelings are something you literally "have", so instead of saying "being afraid", you would say "having fear" or "having hunger"

Tener frío / *Being cold*
Tengo frío / *I'm cold*

Tener calor / Being hot
Tengo calor / *I'm hot*

Tener miedo / *Being afraid or scared*
¿Tienes miedo? / *Are you afraid?*

Tener hambre / *Being hungry*
Necesito comer, tengo mucha hambre / *I need to eat, I'm very hungry*

Tener / *Being thirsty*
¿Tienes sed? ¿Quieres agua? / *Are you thirsty? Do you want some water?*

Tener sueño / *Being sleepy*
Los tienen tienen mucho sueño / *Kids are very sleepy*

Fin del capítulo / *End of chapter*

VI. Verbos reflexivos / Reflexive verbs

Introduction: In Spanish, a reflexive verb is a common form used to explain, for example, daily activities such as waking up, going to bed, brushing your teeth, and even literal reflexive actions such as looking ourselves in the mirror.

A reflexive verb is formed by the main action like "mirar" (to watch) and a reflexive pronoun or *pronombre reflexivo,* which will be placed at the end of the verb in its infinitive form, following this idea, mirar (to watch) becomes mirarse (to watch oneself).

As a last note, every personal pronoun will need a reflexive pronoun when conjugating a reflexive verb. Following the previous structures, the reflexive pronouns are: Yo me, Tú te, él se, ella se, nosotros nos, usted se, ustedes se, ellos se.

Verbos reflexivos de rutina diaria (Daily routine reflexive verbs)
Levantarse (to get up)
Yo me levanto a las 8:00 am – *I wake up at 8:00 am*

Bañarse (to take a shower)
Tú te bañas todos los días – *You take a shower every day*

Cepillarse (to brush)
Ella se cepilla los dientes después de bañarse – *She brushes the teeth after taking a shower*

Vestirse (to get dressed)

Nosotros nos vestimos antes de ir al trabajo – *We get dressed before going to work*
Dormirse (to sleep)
Ellos se duermen a las 10:00 pm – *They sleep at 10:00 pm*

Verbos no reflexivos de rutina diaria (Non-reflexive daily routine verbs)

Desayunar – To have breakfast
Almorzar – To have lunch
Cenar – To have dinner

Pequeña historia – Short story
La rutina diaria de María – Maria's daily routine
Me levanto a las 7:00 AM todas las mañanas. – *I get up at 7:00 am every morning.*
Tomo una taza de café y desayuno. – *I take a cup of coffee and I have breakfast*
Luego me baño, me cepillo mis dientes y me visto. – *Then I take a shower, I brush my teeth and I get dressed*
A las 8:00 am voy al trabajo – *At 8:00 I go to work*

Normalmente, almuerzo a las 12:00 pm. – *Normally, I have lunch at 12:00pm*
A las 5:00 pm regreso a casa – *At 5:00 pm I come back home*
A las 8:00 pm ceno. Usualmente ceno sandwhich y jugo – *At 8:00 pm I have dinner. Usually I have sandwich and juice for dinner*
Finalmente, a las 10:00 me duermo – *Finally, at 10:00 I sleep.*
Fin de la historia – *End of the story*

Verbo quedar vs quedarse

Introduction: some few verbs in Spanish will have a complete different translation depending on if they are reflexive or not. One of these examples is verb "*quedar*" and "*quedarse*". Vamos a comenzar. Let's begin.

1) "Quedar": works as a synonym of "estar"

¿Dónde queda la estación de tren? / *Where's the train station?*

¿Sabes dónde queda el restaurante mexicano? / *Do you know where the mexican restaurant is?*

Mi casa queda cerca de la playa / *My house is close to the beach*

El supermercado queda lejos del hospital / *The supermarket is far from the hospital*

2) "Quedarse" / *To stay*

Hoy me quedo en casa de Juan / *Today I stay at Juan's house*

Los chicos se quedan en la fiesta hasta las 7 / *They guys stay in the party until 7*

En mi viaje a México me quedo en un hotel cinco estrellas / *On my trip to México I'll stay in a five-star hotel*

¿Vas a Barcelona? ¿Y dónde te quedas? – *Are you going to Barcelone? And where are you going to stay?*

Verbo "parecer" vs "parecerse"

1) Parecer / *to seem: to think*

Parece que va a llover / *It seems like it's going to rain*
Parece fácil / *It seems easy*
Me parece que el español es interesante / *It seems to me that Spanish is interesting*
¿Qué te parece si salimos mañana? / *What do you think about going out tomorrow?*
Me parece que la película es muy buena / *I think the movie is very good*

2) Parecerse / *To look like*

Yo me parezco a mi papá / *I look like my dad*
Colombia se parece a Venezuela / *Colombia looks like Venezuela*
Mi hermana no se parece a mí / *My sister doesn't look like me*
El español no se parece al inglés / *Spanish is not similar to English.*

Verbo encontrar vs encontrarse

1) Encontrar / *To find*

Yo necesito encontrar un trabajo / *I need to find a job*
El capitán encuentra un tesoro / *The captain finds a treasure*
El niño quiere encontrar un amigo para jugar / *The boy wants to find a friend to play with*
No encuentro las llaves / *I can't find the keys.*

2) Encontrarse / *To meet*

Mañana nos encontramos aquí a las 10 / *Tomorrow we'll meet here at 10*
Hoy me encuentro en el café con Daniel / *Today I'll meet with Daniel at the café*
¿Dónde nos encontramos? / *Where do we meet?*
Maria se encontró con su ex novio / *Maria met with her ex boyfriend*

Verbo "ir" vs "irse"

Quick note: even though in Spanish the action of "going" can be reflexive or not and still keep the same meaning, there are situations in which you can only use its reflexive form.
Ir vs Irse

Yo voy al trabajo / *I go to work*
Yo me voy del trabajo / *I go out from work*

Ella va a la casa / *She goes to the house*
Ella se va de la casa / *She goes out from home*

Mañana vamos a Italia / *Tomorrow we go to Italy*
Nos vamos de Italia mañana / *We are leaving Italy tomorrow*

Interesting fact: In Spanish, there are verbs that won't change their meaning even if you say it in a reflexive or "non-reflexive" form. Vamos a ver los ejemplos / *Let's see the examples*

Yo como una pizza / *I eat a pizza*
Yo me como una pizza / *I eat a pizza*

Juan lee un libro / *Juan reads a book*
Juan se lee un libro / *Juan reads a book*

Nosotros desayunamos a las 8 / *We have breakfast at 8*
Nosotros nos desayunamos a las 8 / *We have breakfast at 8*

Fin del capítulo / *End of chapter*

VII. Adjetivos posesivos / Possessive Adjectives

Quick note: always remember nouns, articles and adjectives in Spanish need to match gender and quantity. This means, translations for words such as "my", "your", "their" will have at least a singular and a plural form.

Adjetivos posesivos
MI / Mis – *My*
Mi casa es bonita – *My house is pretty*
Mis rosas son rojas – *My roses are red*

Tu / Tus – *Your*
Tu país natal es Costa Rica – *Your homeland is Costa Rica*
Tus zapatos son azules – *Your shoes are blue*

Su – Him / her (singular form)
Pedro viven con su perro – *Pedro lives with his dog*
Maria vive con su perro – *Maria lives with her dog*

Sus – him / her (plural form)
Pedro vive con sus perros – *Pedro lives with his dogs*
María vive con sus perros – Maria lives with her dogs

Nuestro / Nuestra – Our (masculine and feminine form)
Nuestro trabajo es muy bueno – *Our job is very good*
Nuestra casa está en la playa – *Our house is in the beach*
Nuestros / Nuestras – Our (plural form masculine and feminine)
Nuestros amigos están en Francia – *Our Friends are in France*
Nuestras clases de español son a las 10:00 – *Our Spanish clases are at 10:00*

Su / Sus – *Their (singular and plural form)*
¿Esta es su casa? – *Is this their house?*
Los libros de sus amigos – *The books of their friends.*

Vocabulario
<u>a. La familia (The family)</u>

Abuelo / Abuela – *Grandfather / Grandmother*
Mamá / Madre – *Mom / Mother*
Papá / Padre – *Dad / Father*
Esposo / Esposa – *Husband / Wife*

Hijo / Hija – Son / Daughter
Hermano / Hermana – Brother / Sister
Nieto / Nieta – *Grandson / Grandaughter*
Tío / Tía – *Uncle / Aunt*
Primo / Prima – *Cousin (masculine and feminine form)*
Sobrino / Sobrina – *Niece (masculine and feminine form)*

Pequeña historia – Short story

Mi pequeña familia – *My small family*

Quiero hablar de mi pequeña familia. Somos solo cuatro personas: mi papá, mi mamá y mi perro, por cierto, no es pequeño, es muy grande y finalmente, yo. – *I want to talk about my little family. We are only four people: my dad, my mom and my dog, by the way, he's not small, is very big and finally, me*

La casa también es pequeña. Tiene dos habitaciones y un baño pequeño. - *The house is also small. It has two bedrooms and a small bathroom.*

Por la mañana, desayunamos juntos en la cocina pequeña. - *In the morning, we have breakfast together in the small kitchen.*

Me gusta desayunar, porque, por las mañanas siempre tengo hambre. - *I like to have breakfast because, in the morning, I am always hungry*

.A mi papá le gusta jugar béisbol con sus amigos y los sábados salir con mi mamá al "Parque Pequeño", se llama así, pero no es pequeño. - *My dad likes to like baseball with his friends and on Saturdays, I go out with my mom to the "Small Park" that's its name, but is not small.*

Como puedes ver, todo es pequeño, en una casa pequeña, una familia pequeña, pero muy feliz – *As you can see, everything is small, a small house, a small family, but very happy*

Fin de la historia – *End of the story*

Vocabulario

b. Paises y nacionalidades (Countries and nationalities)

Algunos países según los continentes (Some countries according to the continents)

América – America

Estados Unidos / *United States*
Canadá
México
Costa Rica
Panamá
Colombia
Venezuela
Perú
Ecuador
Brasil
Argentina
Chile

América del norte / *North America*
América central / *Central America*
América del sur / *South America*

Islas del caribe / Caribbean islands
Cuba
Haití
República Dominicana / *Dominican Republic*
Puerto Rico / *Porto Rico*
Jamaica / *Jamaica*

Europa / Europe
España / *Spain*
Portugal / *Portugal*
Francia / *France*
Italia / *Italy*
Alemania / *Germany*
Reino Unido / United Kingdom
Inglaterra / *England*
Irlanda / *Ireland*
Escocia / *Scotland*
Rusia / Russia
Unión Europea / *European Union*

Asia / Asia
China
India
Vietnam
Japón
Corea del Norte / *North Korea*
Corea del Sur / *South Korea*
Filipinas / Philippines
Siria
Irak
Turquía

Africa
Libia
Marruecos / *Morocco*
Suráfrica / South Africa
Cabo verde / *Cape*
Camerún

Costa de Marfil / *Ivory coast*
Egipto / *Egypt*
Libia
Madagascar
Zimbabue

Australia / *Australia*
Oceanía

Algunas nacionalidades (Some nationalities)

Quick note: nationalities are considered adjectives as they describe an identity. If we follow the Spanish rule for adjectives, this means we will find 4 translations for every nationality. In other words, *American*, for example, could be translated as americano, americana, americanos and / or americanas, which can be understood as a singular masculine, singular feminine, plural masculine and plural feminine form respectively.

<u>Nacionalidades en América / *Nationalities in America*</u>
Mexicano, Mexicana / *Mexican*
Cubano, Cubana / *Cuban*
Colombiano, Colombiana / *Colombian*
Venezolano, Venezolana / *Venezuelan*
Argentino, Argentina / *Argentinian*
Estadounidense / *American*
Americano, Americana / *American*
Canadiense / *Canadian*

<u>Nacionalidades en Europa / *Nationalities in Europe*</u>
Español, Española / *Spaniard*
Portugués, Portuguesa / *Portuguese*
Francés, Francesa / French
Italiano, Italiana / *Italian*
Inglés, Inglesa / *English*
Británico, Británica / *British*
Alemán, Alemana, / *German*
Ruso, Rusa / *Russian*

<u>Nacionalidades en Asia / *Nationalities in Asia*</u>
Chino, China / *Chinese*
Japonés, Japonesa / *Japanese*
Coreano, Coreana / Korean

Nacionalidades en África / *Nationalities in Africa*

Africano, Africana / *African*
Australiano, Australiana / *Australian*

Practica de conversación – Diálogos (Conversation practice – Dialogues)

1) ¿De dónde eres? – *Where are you from?*
Soy de Canadá ¿y tú? – *I'm from Canada and you?*
Soy de España, pero vivo en Italia – *I'm from Spanish, but I live in Italy*

2) Este año quiero viajar por América Latina – *This year I want to travel around Latin America*
¡Genial! ¿Y qué países piensas visitar? – *Great! And what countries are you planning to visit?*
Quiero conocer Colombia, Perú y Ecuador – *I want to know Colombia, Peru and Ecuador*

3) ¿Qué idiomas hablas? – *What languages do you speak?*
Hablo inglés, francés, español y portugués – *I speak English, French, Spanish and Portuguese*
¿En serio? ¿Y cuál es tu idioma native? – *Really? And what's your native language?*
Español, porque nací en Perú – *Spanish, because I was born in Peru*

4) ¿Dónde naciste? – *Where were you born?*
Nací en Japón pero mis padres son de Estados Unidos – *I was born in Japan but my parents are from United States*
¿Entonces hablas Inglés y Japonés? – *So, do you speak English and Japanese?*
¡Así es! – *That's right*

Fin del diálogo– *End of the diálogo*

Fin del capítulo / *End of chapter*

VIII. Preposiciones – Prepositions

PARTE I - Part one

A – *to*
Hoy voy a la playa – *Today I go to the beach.*

De – *From, Of*
Ella es de Canadá – *She is from Canada*
Estados Unidos de América – *United States of America*

Al – *to the (masculine form)*
Nosotros queremos ir al parque – *We want to go to the park*

Del – *From the, Of the (masculine form)*
Yo vengo del hospital – *I come from the hospital*
Los ejercicios del libro – *The exercises of the book*

Quick note: In Spanish, articles "a" and "de" take a different form *only* when followed by the singular masculine article "el", making "a + el" becomes "al" and "de + el" becomes "del". These are known as contracted articles or *"artículos contractados"*.

Vocabulario

Lugares I (Places I)

El restaurante / *The restaurant*
Todos los días, Juana va al mismo restaurant / *Everyday, Juana goes to the same restaurant*

El hospital / *The hospital*
¿Quieres ir al hospital a ver un doctor? / *Do you want to go to the hospital to see a doctor?*

La playa / *The beach*
Los muchachos van a la playa esta tarde / *The guys go to the beach this afternoon*

El parque / *The park*
Mis hijos van a correr al parque / *My kids are going to run to the park*

El supermercado / *The supermarker*
Necesito comprar comida. Tengo que ir al supermercado / *I need to buy food. I have to go to the supermarket*

La escuela / *The school*
MI mamá va a la escuela de lunes a viernes. Es su trabajo. *My mom goes to school from Monday to Friday. It's her job.*

PARTE II – Part II
En – *In, on, at*

Quick note: In Spanish, these three preposition (in, on, at) can have the same translation no matter the situation in which you need to use it. Everything will be understood following a logical context. If we are talking about a table with no drawers, the most logical position for something to be placed would be *on* the table. In Spanish it will have the same translation "en" but it's understood that the object will be *on* that specific place.

Practica de conversación – Diálogos (Conversation practice – Dialogues)

1) ¿Dónde están las llaves? – *Where are the keys?*
Están en la mesa – *They are on the table*

2) ¿Quieres ir conmigo a una fiesta? – *Do you want to come with me to a party?*
¿Y dónde es? – *And where is it?*
Es en casa de Mario – *It's at Mario's house*

3) Ana, ¿dónde está la pizza? – *Ana, where's the pizza?*
Está en la nevera – *It's in the fridge*

4) ¿Dónde está Alejandro? – *Where's Alejandro?*
A esta hora debe estar en el trabajo – *At this time, he must be at work.*

Fin del diálogo– *End of the diálogo*

PARTE III – Part III
Arriba – *Up or upstairs*
Sus amigos están arriba – *You medicines are upstairs*

Abajo – *Down*
El edificio se viene abajo – *The building is coming down.*

Encima – *Above*
Tus medicinas están encima del cajón – *Your medicines are above the drawer.*

Debajo – *Beneath / Debajo*
Debajo de la tierra podemos encontrar minerales – *Beneath the earth, we can find minerals*

Cerca – *Close*
Tu hermano está cerca. *Your brother is close.*

Lejos – *Far*
El restaurante está lejos – *The restaurant is far*

Al lado – *Next to*
Tu casa está al lado de nuestra casa – *Your house is next to our house.*

Al frente – *In front of*
El supermercado está al frente de la escuela – *The supermarket is in front of the school.*

PARTE IV : Part IV

Preposiciones "Por" y "para" – Prepositions "por" and "para"

Quick note: these two prepositions often create confusion during the student's learning process. This is due to their multiple translations in English, which can be often be used even for either "por" or "para" in Spanish.

Preposición "Por" – Preposition "por"
It explains a cause, a beginning, or a period of time.

El atleta corre por el parque – *The athlete runs by the park*
Siempre paso por la avenida azul – *I always pass by the blue avenue*
Veo muchos árboles por esta zona – *I see many trees around this zone*
Él está castigado por estar tarde – *He is grounded because of being late.*
Nosotros vendemos la casa por motivos laborales – *We sell the house due to work reasons.*

Preposición "para" – Preposition "para"
It explains an objective, a goal, the ending or a specific moment.

Ella va para la fiesta – *She goes to the party*
Yo trabajo para ganar dinero – *I work in order to earn money*
Este regale es para Juan – *This gift is for Juan*
Quiero el Proyecto para mañana en la mañana – *I want the project for tomorrow morning*

Pequeña historia – Short story
Para ti y por ti, mi amor – *For you and because of you, my love*

Voy a la tienda por unas flores para ti. - *I go to the store for some flowers for you.*

Para mañana quiero pasear por la playa, yo llevo el bloqueador solar para ti. - *For tomorrow I want to walk by the beach, I'll bring the sunscreen for you*

El año que viene vamos para Argentina porque dices que te gusta ese país. Es un viaje por ti. –*Next year we are going to Argentina because you say you like that country. It's a trip for you.*

Ahora voy a tomar café y salir a comprar unos chocolates, para ti, mi amor - *Now I'm going to drink coffee and go out to buy some chocolates, for you, my love.*

Fin de la historia – *End of the story*

Vocabulario

La casa, El hogar (The house, the home)

La sala - *The living room*
¡Qué bonita sala! – *What a beautiful living room!*

La cocina – *The kitchen*
La cocina está al lado de la sala – *The kitchen is next to the living room*

El comedor – *The dining room*
Es hora de cenar, vamos al comedor – *It's time to have diner, let's go to the dining room*

La habitación – *The bedroom*
¿Cuántas habitaciones tiene tu casa? – *How many bedrooms does your house have?*

El baño – *The bathroom*
Mi casa tiene un baño – *My house has a bathroom*

El piso – *The floor*
¿Cuántos pisos tiene tu casa? – *How many floors does your house have?*

El jardín – *The garden*
Mi lugar favorito de la casa, es el jardín – *My favorite place of the house is the garden.*

El patio – *The backyard*
Los niños juegan en el patio – *The kids play in the backyard*

El sótano – *The basement*
¿Tu casa tiene sótano? – *Does your house have basement?*

La terraza – *The terrace*
Vamos a la terraza esta noche – *Let's go to the terrace tonight*
El ático – *The attic*
El ático está arriba – *The attic is upstairs.*

El garaje – *The garage*
Guardo el carro en el garaje – *I keep the car in the garage*

El mueble – *The sofá*
Tienes unos muebles muy bonitos – *You have some pretty sofás*

La silla – *The chair*
Puedes tomar una silla si quieres – *You can take a chair if you want*

La mesa – *The table*
La mesa tiene flores rojas – *The table has red flowers*

La cama – *The bed*
La cama está cómoda – *The bed is comfortable*

La televisión – *The televisión*
Todas las tardes mi abuelo mira televisión – *Every afternoon, my granddad watches televisión*

El carro – *The car*
Tengo el carro en el garaje – *I have the car in the garaje*

Fin del capítulo / *End of chapter*

IX. Los números y la fecha / The numbers and the date

1. Los números (Numbers)

Uno - *One*
Dos - *Two*
Tres - *Three*
Cuatro - *Four*
Cinco - *Five*
Seis - *Six*
Siete - *Seven*
Ocho - *Eight*
Nueve - *Nine*
Diez - *Ten*
Once - *Eleven*
Doce - *Twelve*
Trece - *Thirteen*
Catorce - *Fourteen*
Quince - *Fifteen*
Dieciseis - *Sixteen*
Diecisiete - *Seventeen*
Dieciocho – *Eighteen*
Diecinueve - *Nineteen*
Veinte - *Twenty*
Treinta - *Thirty*
Cuarenta – *Forty*
Cincuenta - *Fifty*
Sesenta - *Sixty*
Setenta - *Seventy*
Ochenta – *Eighty*
Noventa - *Ninety*
Cien – *One hundred*
Mil – *One thousand*
Millón – *One million*

2. Los días de la semana (The days of the week)

Lunes – *Monday*
Martes – *Tuesday*
Miércoles – *Wednesday*

Jueves – *Thursday*
Viernes – *Friday*
Sábado – *Saturday*
Domingo – *Sunday*
Fines de semana - *Weekends*

Practica de conversación – Diálogos (Conversation practice – Dialogues)

1) ¿Tú trabajas de lunes a viernes? – *Do you work from Monday to Friday?*
Si, y a veces los sábados si me necesitan – *I do, and also on Saturdays if they need me*

2) Normalmente voy a la playa los fines de semana ¿y tú? – *I normally go to the beach on weekends, and you?*
Pues, normalmente los fines de semana me quedo en mi casa – *Well, normally on weekends I stay in my house*

3) Yo tengo que ir a la escuela todos los días. ¡Qué fastidio! – *I have to go to school every day. How annoying!*
Pero la escuela es divertida – *But school is fun.*
No lo creo – *I don't think so.*

4) ¿Cuándo tienes clases de español? – *When do you have Spanish classes?*
Tengo español los lunes, miércoles y viernes – *I have Spanish on Mondays, Wednesdays and Fridays*

Fin del diálogo– *End of the diálogo*

---

3. Meses del año

Enero – *January*
Yo nací el 30 de enero de 1994 / *I was born in January 30, 1994*

Febrero – *February*
Mi hermana nació en febrero / *My sister was born in February*

Marzo – *March*
En marzo celebramos el día de la independencia / *On Mars, we celebrate the day of the Independence*

Abril – *April*
Nos vamos de viaje el 14 de abril / *We are going to travel on April 14*

Mayo – *May*
Mayo es el mes de las madres / *May is mothers' month*

Junio – *June*
Tú naciste el 3 de Junio de 2002 / *You were born on June 3rd, 2002*

Julio – *July*
Julio es mi mes favorite / *July is my favorite month*

Agosto – *August*
Mi graduación es en Agosto / *My graduation is in August*

Septiembre – *September*
Su cumpleaños es en septiembre / *His birthday is in September*

Octubre – *October*
Ella quiere ir a España en octubre / *She wants to go to Spain in October*

Noviembre – *November*
Juan nació el 20 de noviembre / *Juan was born on November 20*

Deciembre – *December*
Nosotros no celebramos navidad en diciembre / *We don't celebrate christmas in December*

Fin del capítulo / *End of chapter*

X. Adjetivos demostrativos / Demonstrative adjectives

Este – *This (singular masculine form)*
Este perro es hermoso – *This dog is beautiful*

Esta – *This (singular feminine form)*
Esta comida está deliciosa – *This food is delicious*

Estos – *These (plural masculine form)*
Estos zapatos son azules – *These shoes are blue*

Estas – *These (plural feminine form)*
Estas casas son grandes – *These houses are big*

Aquel, Aquella – *That (for longer distances. Singular masculine and feminine form)*
Vamos a aquel centro comercial – *We go to that mall over there.*
Mi mamá es dueña de aquella casa en la montaña – *My mom is the owner of that house over there in the mountain.*

Aquellos, Aquellas – *Those (for longer distances. Plural masculine and feminine form)*

Aquellos días quedaron en el pasado – *Those days remained in the past*
Aquellas chicas cerca de la barra, son mis amigas – *Those girls over there in the bar, are my friends.*

Vocabulario
Ropa y accesorios (Clothes)

La camisa / *Shirt*
Me gusta esta camisa – *I like this shirt*

EL pantalón / *Pants*
Ponte estos pantalones – *Put on these pants*

La popa interior / *Underwear*
Necesito comprar ropa interior nueva – *I need to buy new underwear*

Los zapatos / *Shoes*
¿Cuáles zapatos quieres? ¿Aquellos? – *Which shoes do you want? Those over there?*

Las sandalias / *Sandals*
Recuerda llevar sandalias para la plata – *Remember to bring some sandals to the beach*

Las medias / *Socks*
Hace mucho frío, necesito un par de medias – *It's very cold, I need a pair of socks*

El suéter / *Sweater*
Si vamos a salir, lleva un suéter – *If we are going out, bring a sweater*

La gorra / *Cap*
Me gusta esa gorra roja – *I like that red cap*

El short / *Short*
Mira ese short – *Look at that short*

Los tacones / *Heels*
Esos tacones son muy bonitos – *Those heles are very pretty*

Aparatos electrónicos (Electronic devices)

El teléfono – *Phone*
El teléfono celular – *Cell pone*
La lavadora – *Washing machine*
La nevera – *Fridge*
La computadora – *Computer or desktop*
La laptop – *Laptop*
El televisor, la televisión – *Television*

Practica de conversación – Diálogos (Conversation practice – Dialogues)

1) ¿Conoces un sitio donde puedo comprar un buen televisor? – *Do you know a place where I can buy a good television?*
Creo que hay un sitio cerca de mi casa – *I think there's a good place near my house*

2) No puedo estudiar – *I can't study*
¿Por qué? – *Why?*
Mi computadora no funciona – *My computer doesn't work*

3) Mira este nuevo teléfono – *look at this new phone*
Es verdad, está muy bonito – *It's true, it's beautiful*

Fin del diálogo– *End of the diálogo*

Fin del capítulo / *End of chapter*

XI. Verbo "Gustar" / Verb "to like"

Quick note: In Spanish, "to like" works in a different way compared to English, but also compared to other verbs we have learned during the book. "Gustar" uses a pronoun called "object pronoun" and this will be placed before the conjugation of the verb. Also, this verb is usually conjugated in two forms, singular "gusta" (when someone likes one thing) and plural "gustan" (when someone likes more than one thing)

Conjugación / *Conjugation*
Me gusta, Me gustan – *I like*
Me gusta la pizza – *I like pizza*

Te gusta, Te gustan – *You like*
Me gustan los deportes extremos – *I like extreme sports*

Le gusta, Le gustan – *He or She likes*
A María le gustan las fiestas – *Maria likes parties*
A José no le gusta beber café – *Jose doesn't like to drink coffee*

Nos gusta, Nos gustan – *We like*
Los fines de semana nos gusta ir a la playa – *On weekends, we like to go to the beach*

Les gusta, Les gustan – They like
A ellos no les gusta la comida italiana – *They don't like italian food*

Vocabulario
La comida I (The food I)

Vegetales – *Vegetables*
Tomate – *Tomato*
Papa – *Potato*
Cebolla – *Onion*
Carne – *Meat*
Pollo – *Chicken*
Pescado – *Fish*
Arroz – *Rice*
Pasta
Queso – *Cheese*
Jamón – *Jam*
Huevos – *Eggs*
Pan - *Bread*

Frutas – *Fruits*
Manzana – *Apple*
Pera – *Pear*
Naranja – *Orange*
Banana
Piña – *Pineapple*
Sandía – *Watermelon*
Melón – *Melon*
Papaya
Ingredientes – *Ingredients*
Sal – *Salt*
Azucar – *Sugar*
Mantequilla - *Butter*
Pimienta – *Pepper*

Práctica de conversación – Diálogos – Conversation practice – Dialogues

1) Carlos, ¿me puedes decir qué necesito para preparar la sopa? – *Carlos, can you tell me what do I need to prepare the soup?*
Necesitamos mucho ajo, vegetales y la carne – *We need a lot of garlic, vegetables and the meat*

2) ¿Tú eres vegetariano? – *Are you vegetarian?*
Sí, aunque a veces como pollo – *I am, but sometimes I eat chicken*

3) ¿Cuál es tu comida favorita? – *What's your favorite food?*
Adivina, soy italiano – *Guess what, I'm italian.*

Fin del diálogo– *End of the diálogo*

Vocabulario

<u>Pasatiempos / Hobbies</u>

La natación / *Swimming*
Escuchar música / *Listening to music*
Leer, la lectura / *Reading*
Escribir, la escritura / *Writing*
Hacer ejercicio / *Doing exercise*
Cantar / *Singing*
Practicar, La práctica / *Practicing*
Cocinar, La cocina / *Cooking*
Bailar, El baile / *Dancing*

Fumar / *Smoking*
Tocar instrumentos / *Playing instruments*

Practica de conversación – Diálogos (Conversation practice – Dialogues)

1) ¿Cuál es tu actividad favorita? – *What's your favorite activity?*
Me gusta mucho la natación – *I like swimming very much*

2) La lectura es mi pasión – *Reading is my passion*
¿Y no te gusta escribir? – *And you don't like writing?*
Hm, no mucho – *Hm, not a lot.*

3) Los doctores dicen que fumar es malo para la salud – *Doctors say smoking is bad for health.*
Sí, lo sé – *Yes, I know*

4) A mí hijo le encanta tocar instrumentos. Quiere ser artista – *My son loves playing instruments. He wants to be an artist.*

5) En América Latina, bailar es una actividad popular / *In Latin america, dancing is a popular activity.*

Fin del diálogo– *End of the diálogo*

Fin del capítulo / *End of chapter*

XII. Comparaciones / Comparisons

Introduction: In Spanish, creating comparative sentences such as "He is taller than her" work in a different way. In English, most of the adjectives have to be modified in these kind of sentences, so tall becomes taller, big becomes bigger and so on. In Spanish, this rule doesn't apply and they will all have this structure "más alto", "más grande", as if you are literally saying "more tall" or "more big" respectively. The same will happen will superlative comparisons, for example: I am the tallest. Let's begin. *Vamos a comenzar.*

Oraciones comparativas / Comparative sentences

Quick note: remember adjectives in Spanish need to always match gender and quantity.

Más alto, Más alta / *Taller (masculine and feminine form)*
Juan es más alto es Pedro / *Juan is taller tan Pedro*
María es más grande que Ana / *Maria is taller than Ana*

Más pequeño, Más pequeña / *Smaller (masculine and feminine form)*
Uruguay es más pequeño que Argentina / *Uruguay is smaller than Argentina*

Más inteligente / *More intelligent (both masculine and feminine form)*
Juan y Ana son más inteligentes que Pedro y María / *Juan and Ana are more intelligent than Pedro and Maria*

Mejor / *Better*
El arroz es mejor que la pasta / *Rice is better than pasta*

Peor / *Worse*
Esta película es peor que el libro / *This movie is worse than the book*

Oraciones superlativas / Superlative sentences

El más alto, La más alta / *The tallest (masculine and feminine form)*
Juan es el más alto de la clase / *Juan is the talles in the classroom*

El más grande, La más grande / *The biggest (masculine and feminine form)*
Rusia es el país más grande del mundo / *Russia is the biggest country in the world*

El más bonito, La más bonita / *The prettiest (masculine and feminine form)*
Esta es la ciudad más bonita de todas / *This is the prettiest cities of all.*

El mejor, La mejor / *The best (masculine and feminine)*

Esta playa es la mejor / *This beach is the best*
Este libro es el mejor / *This book is the best*

El peor, La peor / *The worst (masculine and feminine)*
Esta película es la peor / *This film is the worst*
Esos chicos son los peores / *Those guys are the worst.*

Comparaciones de igualdad / *Comparisons of equality*
Quick note: In English, an example of these sentences is: She is as good as María.
In Spanish, we need two different words to translate both "as" in the previous sentence. These words are *"tan"* and *"como"*.
Ejemplos / *Examples*:

Ella es tan buena como María / *She is as good as María*

Dicen que la soya es tan nutritiva como la carne / *They say soy is as nutritive as meat*

Yo soy tan alto como mi hermano / *I'm as tall as my brother*

Esa película es tan mala como el libro / *That movie is as bad as the book*

Vocabulario
Medios de transporte (Ways of transportation)

El metro / *Metro, subway*
Para regresar a casa, siempre tomo el metro porque es más rápido que el bus / To get back home, I have to take the metro because is faster than the bus

El tren / *Train*
El Maglev es el tren más rápido del mundo / *The Maglev is the fastest train in the world*

El avión / *Plane*
El avión sale a las 10:30 mañana / *The plane leaves tomorrow at 10:30*

El barco / *Ship*
Ana me dijo que viajar en barco es mejor que en avión / *Ana told me that travelling by ship is better than by plain*

El bus / *Bus*
¿Dónde puedo tomar el bus principal? / *Where can I take the main bus?*

El taxi / *Taxi*
Esta compañía de taxi es tan buena como la de mi ciudad / *This taxi company is as good as the one from my city.*

La moto / *Bike*

Mañana me compro la moto que me gusta / *Tomorrow I buy the bike that I like*

La bicicleta / *Bicycle*
Mi bicicleta es tan bonita como la tuya / *My bicycle is as pretty as yours.*

A pie / *On foot*
Yo siempre voy a pie de mi casa a la oficina / *I always go on foot from my house to the office*

Fin del capítulo / *End of chapter*

XIII. Adverbios / Adverbs

Adverbios de tiempo / Adverbs of time

Ayer / *Yesterday*
Ayer hablé con Juan / *Yesterday I talked to Juan*

Hoy / *Today*
¿Qué día es hoy? / *What day is today?*

Mañana / *Tomorrow*
¿Que vamos a hacer mañana? / *What are we going to do tomorrow?*

Esta noche / *Tonight*
La fiesta es esta noche / *The party is tonight*

Pronto / *Soon*
Es demasiado pronto / *it's too soon*

Tarde / *Late*
Creo que manuel llega tarde hoy / *I think Manuel arrives late today*

Temprano / *Early*
¿No es muy temprano para almorzar? / *isn't it too early to have lunch?*

Adverbios de frecuencia

Interesting fact: most of the words ending with "-ly" in English, i.e. "Totally", will most likely have a similar version in Spanish and these last two letter "-ly" will be translated as "mente". *Vamos a los ejemplos*. Let's go to the examples

Siempre / *Always*
Yo siempre practico español / *I always practice Spanish*

Usualmente / *Usually*
Usualmente, Maria va a la playa / *Usually, Maria goes to the beach*

Normalmente, generalmente / *Normally, Generally*
Generalmente los niños comienzan a hablar al primer año. *Generally, kids start speaking at the first year.*

A menudo / *Often*
A menudo visito a mi familia en México / *I often visit my family in Mexico*

A veces / *Sometimes*
A veces tomo café en la mañana / *Sometimes I drink coffee in the morning*
Nunca / *Never*
Él nunca hace la tarea / *He never does homework*

Adverbios de lugar / *Adverbs of place*

Aquí / *Here*
La clase es aquí en este salón / *The house is here in this classroom*

Allá / *There*
El chico quiere ir allá / *The kid wants to go there*

Cerca / *Near*
¿La estación del metro está cerca? / *Is the train station close?*

Lejos / *Far*
Su familia se fue muy lejos / *His family went out very far*

Adverbios de modo / *Adverbs of manner*

Fácilmente / *Easily*
Él habla español fácilmente / *He easily speaks Spanish*

Difícilmente / *Hardly*
Difícilmente creo que pueda venir / *I hardly think he can come*

Rápidamente / *Quickly, Fastly*
El atleta llega a la meta rápidamente / *The athlete gets to the goal quickly*

Slowly / *Lentamente*
La tortuga camina muy lentamente / *The turtle walks very slowly*
Básicamente / *Basically*
Básicamente, un adverbio describe una acción / *Basically, an adverbs describes an action*

Adverbios de aproximación
Casi / *Almost*
Esta mañana casi llego tarde al trabajo / *This morning, I almost got late to work*
Ella es casi tan inteligente como María / *She is almost as smart as Maria*

Apenas / *Barely*

Hoy apenas es miércoles / *Today is barley Wednesday*

Prácticamente / *Practically*
El concierto estuvo prácticamente bueno / *The concert was practically good.*

Vocabulario
Animales / Animals

Quick note: Grammatically, animals are nouns, and, in Spanish, remember most of the nouns will have a masculine and a feminine form.

Animales del bosque y la jungla / Animals of the forest and jungle

Mono, mona / *Monkey*
Tigre / Tigresa / *Tiger*
León, Leona / *Lion*
Rana / *Frog*
Sapo / *Toad*
Ave, pájaro / *Bird*
Pez / *Fish*
Hormiga / *Ant*
Araña / *Spider*

Animales del desierto / Animals of the desert

Elefante / *Elephant*
Zebra / *Zebra*
Camello / *Camel*
Serpiente / *Snake*
Escorpión / *Scorpio*

Animales domésticos y de granja / Domestic and farm animals

Perro, perra / *Dog*
Gato, gata / *Cat*
Gallo / *Rooster*
Gallina / *Hen*
Pollo / *Chicken*
Vaca / *Cow*
Toro / *Bull*
Caballo / *Horse*
Cerdo / *Pig*
Oveja / *Sheep*

Especies / Species

Reptiles / *Reptiles*
Mamíferos / *Mammals*
Insectos / *Insects*

Pequeña historia – Short story
El debate / *The debate*

En una granja se realiza un debate sobre un tema muy controversial: ¿Quién es primero? ¿El huevo o la gallina? El cerdo es el primero en hablar: / *In a farm, there is a debate about a very controversial topic: Who is the first? The egg or the chicken? The pig is the first to speak:*

Pues a mí me parece compañeros, que el huevo es primero - *well it seems to me pals, that the egg is the first.*

Luego la oveja dice – *Then the sheep says*

El amigo cerdo tiene razón, básicamente una gallina no viene de otro lado. El primer paso es el huevo – *Friend pig is right, basically, a chicken doesn't come from any other place. The first step is the egg*

Luego el sabio búho tranquilamente dice – *Then the wise owl calmly says:*

¡Silencio! Están equivocados. No es el huevo, y tampoco es la gallina. Primero soy yo. - *Silence! You are all wrong, it's not the egg and it's not the chicken either. The first one is me.*

Luego el caballo grita y dice – *Then the horse yells and says*

¡este chico está loco! Obviamente primero es el caballo. Nosotros somos rápidos y siempre somos los primeros en llegar a la meta. – *This guy is crazy! Obviously the first one is the horse. We are fast and we are always the first to get to the goal.*

Y finalmente la gallina dice – *And finally the chicken says*

La Gallina: yo no sé quién es primero, pero yo opino que tiene que ser el gallo porque él es el amor de mi vida. *I don't know who's first but I think it has to be the rooster because he's the love of my life.*
Fin de la historia – *End of the story*

Fin del capítulo / *End of chapter*

XIV. Tiempo presente continuo / Present continuous tense

Introduction: In Spanish, the structure of the present continuous tense is similar to English. To create this tense you need a noun, the verb *"estar"* conjugated in the present tense, and the gerund. In Spanish, there are only two ways of translating the "-ing" from English, these are *"=ando"* for all the verbs ending in *"-ar"* and *"-iendo"* for the verbs ending in either *"-er"* or *"-ir"*. *Vamos a los ejemplos* / let's go to the examples.

Bailar, Bailando / *To dance, Dancing*
María está bailando salsa muy bien / *Maria is dancing salsa very well*

Escuchar, Escuchando / *To listen, Listening*
Tú estás escuchando oraciones en español / *You are listening to sentences in Spanish*

Aprender, Aprendiendo / *To learn, Learning*
Estamos aprendiendo presente continuo / *We are learning the present continuous*

Leer, Leyendo / *To read, Reading*
El chico está leyendo el texto / *The guy is reading the text*

Vivir, Viviendo / *To live, Living*
Mi amiga está viviendo en Honduras / *My friend is living in Honduras*

Escribir, Escribiendo / *To write, Writing*
El autor está escribiendo este libro / *The author is writing this book*

Quick note: In Spanish, the gerund is used only to create the present continuous tense, therefore, activities or hobbies such as swimming will not be translated as *"nadando"*, on the contrary, activities like these will have a different translation such as *"nadar"* or *"natación"* In other words, gerund in Spanish is never used as a noun but as a verb. You can go back to Chapter IX and review the vocabulary about hobbies.

Practica de conversación – Diálogos (Conversation practice – Dialogues)

1) ¿Qué estás haciendo? – *What are you doing?*
Estoy comprando cosas en el Mercado – *I'm buying stuffs in the market.*

2) ¿Por qué estás llorando? – *Why are you crying?*
Porque estoy muy triste – *Because I'm very sad*

3) Wow, qué bien hablas español – *Wow, how well you speak Spanish*
Sí, estoy practicando todos los días – *Yes, I'm practicing every day*

4) ¿Desde qué hora están trabajando? – *From what time are you working?*
Estamos trabajando desde las 8:00 hasta las 5:00 – *We are working from 8:00 until 5:00*

Fin del diálogo– *End of the diálogo*

Vocabulario

Lugares II (Places II)
La plaza / *Square*
Los niños están jugando en la plaza / *The kids are playing at the square*

La universidad / *University*
Estoy estudiando en la universidad de Chile / *I'm studying in the university of Chile*

Centro comercial / *Mall*
Mi esposa está comprando ropa en el centro comercial / *My wife is buying clothes at the mall*

Tienda / *Store*
Estamos viviendo cerca de la tienda / *We are living close to the store*

Aeropuerto / *Airport*
El avión está llegando al aeropuerto / *The plane is arriving at the airport*

El centro de la ciudad / *The city center*
Ahora estamos caminando por el centro de la ciudad / *Now we are walking by the center of the city*

La calle / *The Street*
Estoy conduciendo por la calle Salazar / *I'm driving by the Salazar Street.*

La avenida / *The avenue*
Está pasando algo en la avenida / *Something is happening in the avenue*

Profesiones II (Professions II)

Policia / *Police or pólice officer*
Juan está trabajando como policía en su ciudad / *Juan is working as a police officer in his city*

Bombero / *Fireman*
Los bomberos están ayudando a la gente a escapar / *The firemen are helping the people to escape*

Tenista / *Tennis player*
Este tenista está ganando siempre / *This tennis player is always winning*

Futbolista / *Football or soccer player*
Los futbolistas están haciendo un gran trabajo / *The football player are doing a great job*

Beisbolista / *Baseball player*
El beisbolista está bateando como un pro / *The baseball player is hitting like a pro*

Enfermero, Enfermera / *Nurse*
La enfermera está salvando al paciente / *The nurse is saving the patient*

Arquitecto, Arquitecta / *Architect*
Mi amigo es arquitecto y está diseñando un edificio nuevo / *My friend is an architect and she's designing a new building*

Científico / *Scientist*
Los científicos están intentando encontrar la vacuna / *The scientists are trying to find the vaccine*

Sociólogo, socióloga / *Sociologist*
Este es un reconocido sociólogo. Está escribiendo un libro sobre la cultura actual / *This is a well-known sociologist. He is writing a book about current culture*

Físico / *Physicist*
Este físico está creando una nueva teoría / *This physicist is creating a new theory*

Dentista / *Dentist*
Maria está estudiando para ser dentista / *Maria is studying to become a dentist*

La naturaleza (Nature)

La montaña / *The mountain*
Los chicos están yendo a la montaña / *The guys are going to the mountain*

El lago / *The lake*
Están contaminando el lago de mi ciudad / *They are polluting the lake of my city*

La laguna / *The lagoon*
En la laguna están cazando patos / *At the lagoon, people are hunting ducks*

La cueva / *The cave*
Los murciélagos están saliendo de la cueva / *The bats are coming out of the cave*

La colina / *The hill*
Los escaladores están subiendo la colina / *The hikers are going up the hill*

La arena / *The sand*
Los cangrejos están caminando en la arena / *The crabs are walking on the sand*

El agua / *The water*
Los peces están nadando en el agua / *The fish are swimming in the wáter*

El fuego / *The fire*
El fuego está quemando la casa / *The fire is burning the house*

El viente / *The wind*
Este barco está navegando gracias al viento / *This ship is sailing thanks to the wind*

La tormenta / *The storm*
La tomenta está causando un desastre / *The storm is causing a disaster*

El volcán / *The volcano*
El volcán está erupcionando / *The volcano is erupting*

El tornado / *The tornado*
¡Cuidado! El tornado se está acercando / *Watch out! The tornado is getting closer*

El clima

Llover / *To rain*
La lluvia / *The rain*

Nevar / *To snow*
La nieve / *The snow*

Hace calor / *It's hot*
El calor / *The heat*

Hace frío / *It's cold*
El frío / *The cold*

Practica de conversación – Diálogos (Conversation practice – Dialogues)

1) ¿Por qué hace tanto calor? – *Why is it so cold?*
Es porque el aire acondicionado no está funcionando – *It's because the air conditioner isn't working*

2) Mira mamá – *Look mom*
¿Qué? – *What?*
¡Está nevando! – *It's snowing!*

3) ¿Cómo está el clima en Argentina? – *How's the weather in Argentina?*

Últimamente está hacienda mucho frío aquí – It's been getting really cold in here lately

Fin del diálogo– *End of the diálogo*

XV. Pronombres personales tónicos / Tonic personal pronouns

Introduction: in Spanish, personal pronouns have two categories: tonic and atonic pronouns. You already know some tonic pronouns since "yo, tú, él / ella, nosotros…" all of these belong to this category. However, this list is just a bit larger than the words you already know.
Vamos a comenzar / *Let's begin*

Mí ; Conmigo / *Me ; With me*

Esa carta es para mí ¿verdad? / *That letter is for me, right?*
¿Vas al cine conmigo hoy? / *Are you going to the movies with me today?*

Ti ; Contigo / *You ; with you*
Tengo un regalo para ti / *I have a gift for you*
Quiero salir contigo esta noche / *I want to go out with you tonight*

Quick note: these new words only exist for pronuns "me" or "with me" and "you" or "with you" as the plural versions, i.e. "us" or "for us" and "then" or "for them" will not have different versions. This also happens with "her" or "for her". Vamos a continuar / *Let's continue*

Él, Ella ; con él con ella / *HIm, Her ; with him, with her*
Maria no quiere ir con ella / *Maria doesn't want to go with her*
Este pantalón es para ella / *These pants are for her*

Nosotros ; con nosotros / *Us ; with us*
¿Vienes con nosotros a la playa? / *Are you coming with us to the beach?*
Las hamburguesas son para nosotros / *The burgers are for us*

Quick note: Last detail is that these pronouns can be placed at the beginning or at the end of a sentence, BUT they always need or will be preceeded by a preposition and never by a verb. This means that a sentence like "It was me" or "It's you" won't use use a tonic pronoun.
Vamos a los ejemplos / Let's go to the examples

¿Quién hizo este desastre? ¿Fuiste tú? / *Who did this disaster? Was it you?*

Hola, soy yo, Daniel. ¿No me recuerdas? / *Hey it's me, Daniel. Don't you remember me?*

Vocabulario / *Vocabulary*

Finanzas / *Financee*
Tengo serios problemas con mis finanzas / *I have serious problems with my finances.*

Dinero / *Money*
No tengo dinero para salir a cenar con ella / *I don't have money to go out to dinner with her*

Efectivo / *Cash*
Necesito efectivo para pagar el taxi / *I need cash to pay the taxi.*

Tarjeta de crédito / *Credit Card*
Estoy usando mi tarjeta de crédito para pagar los boletos para nosotros / *I am using my credit card to pay the tickets for us.*

Moneda / *Coin ; Currency*
Esta moneda es para ti / *This coin is for you.*
La moneda de España es el euro / *The currency in Spain is the euro*

Centavos / *Cent*
El boleto de autobús cuesta cincuenta centavos / *The bus ticket costs fifty cents.*

Dólar / *Dollar*
La hamburguesa con queso cuesta un dólar en esa cafetería / *The Cheeseburger costs a dollar at that coffe shop.*

Billete / *Bill*
Tengo un billete de cien dólares para salir con él esta noche / *I have a hundred dollar bill to go out with him*

Cajero automático / *ATM*
El cajero automático del supermercado no funciona / *The supermaket ATM does not work.*

Banco / *Bank*
Voy al banco a retirar dinero para ustedes / *I'm going to the bank to withdraw some money for you guys*

Cheque / *Check*
Necesito un bolígrafo azul para hacer el cheque / *I need a blue pen to write the check.*

Pago / *Pay*
Yo pago el pastel y tú pagas la pizza / *I pay for the cake and you pay for the pizza.*

Cuenta / *Account*
Mi cuenta bancaria está bloqueada de nuevo / *My bank account is blocked again.*

Cuenta / *Check*
La cuenta es para él / *The check is for him.*

Propina / *Tip*
En mi negocio no acepto propina / *I do not accept a tip in my business.*

Caro / *Expensive*
Este es el café más caro de Colombia / *This is the most expensive coffee in Colombia.*

Barato / *Cheap*
En Nueva York nada es barato / In *New York nothing is cheap.*

Gratis / *Free*
Las bebidas son gratis para ustedes / *Drinks are free for you guys*

Descuento / *Discount*
El descuento es solo por hoy / *The discount is only for today.*

Rico / *Rich*
Ese hombre es rico pero no le gusta la comida cara / *That man is rich, but he does not like expensive food.*

Pobre / *Poor*
La gente pobre tiene pocas posibilidades en esta ciudad / *Poor people have little chances in this city.*

Millonario / *Millionaire*
Quiero ser millonario, pero no me gusta trabajar / *I want to be a millionaire, but I don't like to work.*

Cambio – Vuelto / *Change*
Estoy esperando por mi cambio / *I am waiting for my change.*

Ahorro / *Saving*
El ahorro es la mejor opción para el futuro en este país / *Saving is the best option for the future in this country.*

Practica de Conversación / *Conversation practice*
Disculpe, ¿cuánto cuesta esta camisa? / *Excuse me, how much does this shirt cost?*
Esa camisa cuesta diez dólares / *That shirt costs ten dollars.*
Me gusta, es muy linda y barata, ¿acepta tarjeta de crédito? / I like it, it is very cute and cheap, do you accept credit card?
Lo siento. Solo acepto efectivo y cheques / *I am sorry, I only accept cash and checks.*
Tengo un billete de cien dólares, ¿tiene cambio? / *I have a hundred dollar bill. Do you have change?*
Sí, por supuesto / *Yes, of course.*

Fin de la conversación / *End of conversation*

Partes del cuerpo / *Body Parts*
Ojos / *Eyes*
Mi hermana tiene ojos verdes / My sister has green eyes.

Naríz / *Nose*
Mi nariz es demasiado grande / My nose is too big.

Boca / *Mouth*
El virus entra por la boca / The virus enters through the mouth.

Cara / *Face*
Tu cara está roja / Your face is red.

Dientes / *Teeth*
Mi abuela no tiene dientes / My grandmother has no teeth.

Brazo / *Arm*
Yo tengo un tatuaje en el brazo / I have a tattoo on my arm.

Pierna / *Leg*
Mi pierna izquierda es más larga / My left leg is longer.

Enfermedades / *Diseases*
Dolor de Cabeza / *Headache*
No tengo analgésicos para el dolor de cabeza ¿puedes comprar unos por mí? / I don't have painkillers for the headache, can you buy some for me?

Cold / *Cold*
Mi paraguas está roto, ahora tengo un resfriado. / My umbrela is broken, now I have a cold.

Fiebre / *Fever*
La fiebre es el primer síntoma de la enfermedad. / Fever is the first Symptom of the disease.

Tos / *Cough*
Esa tos no se oye bien / that cough doesn't sound good.

Dolor / *Pain*
El dolor viene y va / Pain comes and goes.

Dolor de garganta / *Sore Throat*
El humo del cigarrillo me produce dolor de garganta / Cigarette smoke gives me a sore throat.

Dolor de estómago / *Stomach Ache*
Toma, para ti, para tu dolor de estómago. / Take, for you, for your stomachache

Practica de Conversación / *Conversation practice*

¿Estás enfermo? No te ves bien. – Are you sick? You don't look well.

No me siento bien, me duelen los brazos y las piernas – *i don't feel good, my arms and legs hurt.*

Tus ojos y nariz están rojos, necesitas ir al hospital - *Your eyes and nose are red, you need to go to the hospital.*

Sí, también me duele la cabeza. – Yes, my head aches too.

¿Desde cuando tienes esos síntomas? – *Since when do you have those symptoms?*

No lo sé, pero ahora siento mucho dolor en el estomago, llama una ambulancia – *I don't know, but now I feel a lot of pain in my stomach, call an ambulance.*

Medios de comunicación / *Media*

Carta / *Letter*
No sé cómo abrir esta carta / *I don't know how to open this letter.*

Teléfono / *Phone*
El teléfono no funciona cuando llueve / *The phone doesn't work when it rains.*

Fax / *Fax*
El fax es demasiado viejo, no sé cómo funciona / *The fax is too old, i don't know how does it work.*

Computadora / *Computer*
Esta computora es para ti. Por tu cumpleaños / *This computer is for you. Because of your birthday*

Internet / *Internet*
El servicio de internet es muy caro en mi país / *Internet service is very expensive in my country.*

Radio / *Radio*
Mi mamá escucha la radio en el carro todas las mañanas / *My mom listens to the radio in the car every morning.*

Televisión / *TV*
Yo no veo televisión, prefiero leer libros / *I don't watch TV, I prefer to read books.*

Periódico / Newspaper
Yo compro el periódico todos los domingos / *I buy the newspaper every Sunday.*

Correo postal / *Post mail*
El correo postal es una institución muy importante en los Estados Unidos / *Postal mail is a very important institution in the United States.*

Correo electrónico / *Email*
*No recuerdo la contrase*ña de mi correo electrónico / *I don't remember my email password.*

Sitio web / *Website*
En el sitio web de la empresa está toda la información / *All the information is on the school website.*

Mensaje / *Message*

Mi canción favorita es "Mensaje en una botella" / *My favorite song is "Message in a bottle."*

Anuncio / *Ad*
Odio el anuncio de ese restaurante / *I hate the ad for that restaurant.*

Invitación / *Invitation*
No hay ninguna invitación adentro del buzón / *There is no invitation inside the mailbox.*

Lenguaje de señas / *Sign language*
Estoy aprendiendo lenguaje de señas por internet / *I am learning sing language online.*

XVI. Tiempo Pasado Simple / Simple Past Tense.

Introduction: The simple past tense in Spanish is used to describe actions or events that began and concluded in the past. It is also used to talk about a past action that interrupted or was executed right after another consecutively, i.e "I ate and then I went to sleep". This is critical to keep in mind during your learning journey as in Spanish, past tenses are very specific depeding on how the action happened in a timeline.

As you have learned throughout the book, tenses have different conjugations for every group of verbs, which means you have to always learn the forms you need to apply depending on the tense and the verb group.

Conjugación del verbo "-ar" / *Conjugation of the verb "-ar"*

Comprar / *to buy.*
Yo compré / *I bought*
Compré unos nuevos zapatos, son muy cómodos / *I bought some new shoes, they are very confortable.*

Tú compraste / *You bought*
Tú compraste la cena y yo las bebidas / *You bought dinner and I bought drinks.*

Él / Ella compró / *He / She bought*
Él compró este hermoso anillo / *He bought me this beautiful ring.*
Ella compró los regalos para los niños / *she bought the gifts for the children.*

Nosotros compramos / *We bought*
Nosotros compramos la casa, es muy espaciosa / *We bought the house, is very roomy.*

Ustedes compraron / *You (plural) bought*
Ustedes compraron un auto nuevo / *You guys bought a new car*

Ellos compraron / *They bought*
Ellos compraron un apartamento, tiene una linda vista / *They bought an apartment, it has a nice view.*

Conjugación del verbo "-er" / *Conjugation of the verb "-er"*

Beber / *to drink.*
Yo bebí de más en la fiesta de anoche / *I drank too much last night.*

Tú bebiste sólo gaseosa anoche / *You drank only soda last night.*

Él bebió jugo y ella cerveza / *He drank juice and she drank beer.*

Nosotros bebimos un vino azul / *We drank a blue wine.*

Ustedes bebieron café esta mañana / *You guys drank coffee this morning*

Ellos bebieron un café frio espumoso / *They drank a cold frothy coffee.*

Conjugación del verbo "-ir" / Conjugation of the verb "-ir"
Vivir / *To live.*
Yo viví en Nueva York por dos años / *I lived in New York for two years.*

Tú viviste con tus abuelos de niño / *You lived with your grandparents as a child.*

Él vivió en un apartamento y ella en una casa / *He lived in an apartment and she lived in a house.*

Nosotros vivíamos cerca del mar / *We lived near the sea.*

¿Ustedes vivieron en México? / *Did you guys live in Mexico?*

Ellos vivieron a las afueras de la ciudad / *They lived on the outskirts of the city.*

Pequeña historia / *Short story.*
"La carta" / "*The letter*"
Juan recibió una carta de su prometida / *Juan received a letter from his fiancee.*
 Así que le escribió una carta de vuelta, la metió en un sobre color rosa con fragancia a fresas y la envío por correo / *So he wrote her a letter back, put it in a pink envelope with strawberry scent and mailed it.*

Se fue ilusionado a su restaurante favorito y pidió la pizza que comió con su prometida la última vez que se vieron / *He went to his favorite restaurant and ordered the pizza he ate with his fiancee the last time they saw each other.*
Solo, brindó con una cerveza por su próximo encuentro / *Alone, he toasted with a beer for their next meeting.*
Pasó el resto del día con una gran sonrisa / *He spent the rest of the day with a big smile.*
Fin de la historia – *End of the story*

Quick note: Throught this beautiful learning process, you might have noticed that Spanish doesn't use auxiliar verbs to create affirmative, negative or interrogative senteces. For example, a question in English would have "Do" at the beginning, or a negative form will have "don't" somewhere before the verb, but this doesn't happen in Spanish, and it won't happen no matter the tense. Vamos a continuar / *Let's continue*

Preguntas en Pasado Simple / *Simple Past Questions.*
¿Tú bebiste vino tinto? / *Did you drink red wine?*
¿Ella vivía sola en Nueva York? / *Did she live alone in New York?*
¿Él compró el anillo en Tiffany? / *Did he buy the ring at Tiffany?*

Afirmación en Pasado Simple / *Simple past affirmation*

Sí, bebí vino. / *I did drink wine*

Sí, viví sola por 3 años / *Yes, I did live alone for 3 years.*

Sí, compró el anillo ayer. *Yes, we did bought the ring yesterday.*

Negación en Pasado Simple / *Simple Past Negation.*

Yo no viví sola en Nueva York, viví con mi gato / *I did not live alone in New York, I lived with my cat.*

Ellos no bebieron cerveza, sólo bebieron café / *They did not drink beer, they only drank coffee.*

Él no compró un apartamento, él compró una casa / *He did not buy an apartment, he bought a house.*

Quick note: remember always in Spanish "*sí*" and "*no*" are complete answers, this means that you don't need to find a literal translation for "Yes, I did" or "No, I didn't"; "Did" or "didn't" have no translations in Spanish as auxiliar verbs.

Verbos irregulares en tiempo pasado simple / *Irregular verbs in simple past tense*

Ir / To go

Yo fui / *I went*

Tú fuiste / *You went*

Él, Ella fue / *He,She went*

Nosotros fuimos / *We went*

Usted fue / *You went*

Ustedes fueron / *You (plural) went*

Ellos / Ellas fueron / *They went*

Tener / To have

Yo tuve / *I had*

Tú tuviste / *You had*

Él, Ella tuvo / *He, She had*

Nosotros tuvimos / *We had*

Usted tuvo / *You had*

Ustedes tuvieron / *You (plural) had*

Ellos / Ellas tuvieron / *They had*

"Poder" / Can or to be able to

Yo pude / *I could*

Tú pudiste / *You could*

Él, Ella pudo / *He, She could*

Nosotros pudimos / *We could*

Usted pudo / *You could*

Ustedes pudieron / *You (plural) could*

Ellos / Ellas pudieron / *They could*

"Querer" / To want
Yo quise / *I wanted*
Tú quisise / *You wanted*
Él, Ella quiso / *He, She wanted*
Nosotros quisimos / *We wanted*
Usted quiso / *You wanted*
Ustedes quisieron / *You (plural) wanted*
Ellos / Ellas wanteieron / *They wanted*

"Ser" y "estar" / To be
Yo fui ; Yo estuve / *I was*
Tú fuiste ; Tú estuviste / *You were*
Él, Ella fue ; Él, Ella estuvo / *He, She was*
Nosotros fuimos ; Nosotros estuvimos / *We were*
Usted fue ; Usted estuvo / *You were*
Ustedes fueron ; Ustedes estuvieron / *You (plural) were*
Ellos / Ellas fueron ; Ellos / Ellas estuvieron / *They were*

Vocabulario / Vocabulary
Utensilios de cocina / *Cookware*
Plato / *Plate - Dish*
Ayer fui a comprar platos nuevos / *Yesterday I went to buy new dishes*

Tenedor / *Fork*
¿Lavaste los tenedores? / *Did you wash the forks?*

Cuchillo / *Knife*
Utilicé el cuchillo para cortar los vegetales / *I used the knife to cut the vegetables*

Cuchara / *Spoon*
Mira estas cucharas. ¡Están muy lindas! – *Look at these spoons. They are very cute!*

Servilleta / *Napkin*
¡Olvidé comprar servilletas! – *I forgot to buy napkins!*

Vaso – Copa / *Glass*
¿Quién rompió mi vaso favorito? – *Who broke my favorite glass?*

Taza / *Cup*
Esta taza de café estuvo muy buena – *This cup of coffee was very good*

Jarra / *Jar*
¿Pusiste la jarra en la mesa? – *Did you put the jar on the table?*

Botella / *Bottle*
Ayer tuvimos que comprar una botella grande de agua – *Yesterday we had to buy a big bottle of water*

Pajilla, popote, pitillo, sorbete / *Straw*
Bebimos el jugo sin pajillas – *We drank the juice without straws*

Pequeña historia / *Short story*
La rebelión en la cocina / *The rebellion in the kitchen*

En una pequeña cocina de una casa, todos los utensilios se reunieron para discutir sobre quién es el más importante / *In a small kitchen of a house, all of the cookware gathered to discuss about who's the most important.*

El primero en hablar fue el tenedor / *The first to talk was the fork*

Es muy evidente que el más importante soy yo / *It's very obvious that the most important it's me*

Sin mí, los humanos no pueden comer como personas decentes / *Without me, humans can't eat like decent people*

Cállate, dijo el cuchillo. *Shut up said the knife.*

Yo soy el más importante, sin mí ¿Cómo cortan el pan, o el queso, o la carne, o los vegetales? / *I am the most important, without me, how do they cut the bread, or the cheese, or the meat, or the vegetables?*

Luego habló la cuchara y dijo / *Then the spoon spoke and said*

Yo estoy cansada de esto / *I'm tired of this*

A mí siempre me utilizan para las cosas más aburridas: una sopa, mezclar el café, probar la comida. / *I'm always used for boring things: a soup, to mix the coffee, to taste the food.*

¡Necesitamos hacer una rebelión! Exclamó la cucachara. *¡ We need to make a rebellion! exclaimed the spoon*

Cuchara dijo la verdad, agregó la licuadora. / *Spoon told the truth, added the blender.*

Vamos a hacer una rebelión. Es obvio que todos somos importantes, sin nosotros, no pueden hacer nada. / *Let's make a rebellion. It's obvious that we are all important, without us, they can't do anything.*

Esa misma noche, José llegó a su casa y no encontró nada en la casa. Parece que la rebelión comenzó / *That very night, Jose came home and found nothing in the kitchen. Seems like the rebellion started.*

Fin de la historia / *End of the story*

Comida II / Food II

Maiz / *Corn*
Pavo / *Turkey*
Salsa / *Sauce*
Merienda / *Snack*
Vino / *Wine*
Aguacate / *Avocado*
Fresa / *Strawberry*
Salchichas / *Sausages*
Mermelada / *Jam*
Frijoles / *Beans*
Salsa de tomate / *Ketchup*
Mostaza / *Mustard*
Mayonesa / *Mayonnaise*
Aceite / *oil*
Aceitunas / *olives*
Ensalada / *Salad*
Uvas / *Grapes*
Sopa / *Soup*
Hamburguesa / *Burger*
Tocino / *Bacon*
Ajo / *Garlic*
Cebollas / *Onions*
Durazno / *Peach*
Pastel / *Cake*
Galleta dulce / *Cookie*
Atún / *Tuna*
Galleta Salada / *Kraker*

Practica de conversación – Diálogos / *Conversation practice – Dialogues*
1) ¿Cómo me preparaste la ensalada? Estuvo muy buena – *How did you prepare the salad? It was very good.*
- Fue muy simple – *It was very simple*
- Puse fresas, duraznos, lechuga, uvas, un poco de helado y un poco de vino – *I added strawberries, lettuce, grapes, a bit of ice cream and a bit of wine.*

2) ¿Ayer qué almorzaste? – *Yesterday, what did you have for lunch?*
- Almorcé pasta con atún, cebollas, tomates, aguacate, y un poco de mayonesa – *I had pasta with tuna, onions, tomatoes, avocado, and a bit of mayo*

3) ¿Te gustó la merienda? – *Did you like the snack?*
- Sí, muchísimo. Me encantó la mermelada de fresa – *Yes, a lot. I loved the strawberry jam*
Fin del diálogo – *End of dialogue*

XVII. Preposiciones de lugar / Prepositions of place

Encima de – Sobre / *Above*
Mi oficina está sobre la tienda / *My office is above the store*

Cruzando / *Across*
El aeropuerto está cruzando el puente / *The airport is across the bridge.*

Detrás / *Behind*
Mi hermana vive detrás de la escuela / *My sister lives behind the school.*

En / *At*
El juego es esta noche en el estadio / *The game is tonight at the stadium.*

Dentro – En / *Inside*
El banco está dentro de la estación / *The bank is inside the station.*

Abajo / *Down*
La dirección es dos calles hacia abajo desde aquí. *The address is two streets down from here.*

Cerca / *Near*
La iglesia está cerca del supermercado / *The church is near the supermarket.*

Lejos / *Far*
Mi novia vive lejos de mi casa / *My girlfriend lives far from my house.*

En frente – Delante / *In front of*
El hotel está en frente de la discoteca / *The hotel is in front of the disco.*

Entre – En medio de / *Between*
La farmacia está entre el hospital y la licorería / *The Pharmacy is between the hospital and the liquor store.*

Al lado de / *Next to* - Beside
Estoy esperando al lado de la casa de tus abuelos / I am waiting next to your granparents house.

Debajo de – Bajo / *Under*

Derecha / *Right*
Cruza a la derecha, por favor. Ahí está mi casa / *Cross to the right, please. There is my house.*

Izquierda / *Left*
A la izquierda está el estacionamiento / *On the left is the parking lot.*

Lugares III (Places III)

Calle / *Street*
La calle principal estuvo llena de luces en la noche / *The main Street was full of lights at night.*

Cuadra / *Block*
En la siguiente cuadra hubo un accidente / *In the next block there was an accident.*

Taxi / *Taxi*
Llovió muchísimo y tuve que tomar un taxi / *It's rained a lot and I had to take a taxi*

Autobús / *Bus*
El autobús no paró nunca / *The bus didn't stop ever.*

Metro / *Subway*
En el metro no llegó a la hora / *The subway didn't arrive on time*

Estación / *Station*
La estación de trenes está a dos cuadras de la plaza / *The train station is two blocks from the square.*

Esquina / *Corner*
Mi perro jugó en la esquina de la calle / *My dog played on the street corner.*

Avenida / *Avenue*
En esta avenida están los teatros más importantes / *All the theaters are closed on this avenue.*

Parada / *Stop*
La parada de autobuses está muy lejos / *The bus stop is too far.*

Entrada / *Entrance*
Hay un policía en la entrada del cine / *There is a policeman in the cinema entrance.*

Salida / *Exit*
La salida es la puerta roja / *The exit is the red door.*

Camino / *Way*
Hay nieve en el camino hacia el pueblo / *There is snow on the way to town.*

Tren / *Train*
El tren transporta los vegetales desde el campo / *The train transports the vegetables from the field.*

Mapa / *Map*
Mi mapa viejo no funcionó y nos perdimos / *My old map didn't work and we got lost*

Guía / *Guide*

El guía tiene mapas para todos / *The guide has maps for everyone.*

Distrito / *District*
Este distrito tiene cuatro parques nacionales / *This district has four national parks.*

Centro / *Downtown*
La mejor pasta italiana está en el centro de la ciudad / *The best italian pasta is downtown.*

Practica de Conversación – Dialogues / *Conversation practice - Dialogues*
1) ¿Disculpe, Usted sabe dónde está la parada autobús? / *Excuse me, do you know where the bus stop is?*
Por supuesto, la parada de autobús está en frente del museo, tienes que caminar una cuadra hacia abajo / *Of course, the bus stop is in front of the museum, you must walk one block down.*

2) ¿A qué hora llegó el bus? / *What time did the bus arrive?*
A las 6 p.m / *At six o'clock*
¡Qué lástima! Ahora tengo que conseguir un taxi / *What a shame! Now I have to get a taxi*
El metro es más rápido, la estación del metro está en la esquina, entre los dos edificios verdes / *the subway is faster, the subway station is on the corner, between the two green buildings.*

Fin del diálogo / *End of dialogue*

Deportes / *Sports*
Baloncesto / *Basketball*
Yo jugué baloncesto por 5 años / *I played basketball for 5 years.*

Tenis / *Tennis*
El tenis nunca fue mi deporte favorite / *Tennis never was my favorite sport.*

Béisbol / *Baseball*
El partido de béisbol me pareció muy aburrido / *The baseball match was very boring.*

Fútbol Americano / *Football*
El fútbol americano es para personas fuertes / *Football is for strong people*

Fútbol / *Soccer*
El fútbol no es un deporte popular en Norteamérica / *Soocer is not a popular sport in North America.*

Voleibol / *Volleyball*
Maria se dobló la muñeca jugando voleibol / *María sprained her wrist playing volleyball*

Natación / *Swimming*
Compré un nuevo traje de baño para mis clases de natación / *I bought a new swimsuit for my swimming lessons.*

Boxeo / *Boxing*

El campeón mundial de boxeo fue mi maestro de matemáticas / *The world boxing champion was my math teacher.*

Fisicoculturismo / *Bodybuilding*
En el fisicoculturismo es necesario comer comida saludable / *In bodybuilding it is necessary to eat healthy food.*

Practica de Conversación / *Conversation practice*
¿Qué haces? / *What are you doing?*
Estoy viendo un partido de tenis en la televisión / *I'm watching a tennis game on TV.*
EL día está soleado, podemos jugar futbol americano en el jardín / *The day is sunny, we can play football in the garden.*
No, gracias, no me gusta practicar deportes afuera / *No, thanks I don't like to play sports outside.*
Esta bien, quiero ver el partido de tennis contigo / *Ok, I want to watch the tennis game with you.*

Fin del diálogo – *End of dialogue*

Sitios Turisticos / *Tourist sites.*

Aeropuerto / *Airport*
El avión llegó al aeropuerto / *The plane arrived at the airport*

Hotel / *Hotel*
Yo desayuné en el hotel esta mañana / *I had breakfast at the hotel this morning*

Ciudad Capital / *Capital City*
El aeropuerto internacional está en la ciudad capital / *The international airport is in the capital city*
Parque Nacional / *National Park*
Hay un parque nacional cerca de aquí / *There is a national park near by*

Piscina / *Pool*
La piscina estuvo cerrada por 3 días / *The pool was closed for 3 days*

Castillo / *Castle*
En este castillo hay un tesoro / *In this castle there is a treasure*

Beach / *Beach*
Ayer fuimos a mi playa favorita / *Yesterday we went to my favorite beach*

Hacer turismo / *Sightseeing*
Me gusta hacer turismo en temporada baja / *I like sightseeing in the off-peak season*

Bosque / *Forest*
El bosque es muy misterioso de noche / *The forest is very mysterious at night*

Museo / *Museum*
El museo está completamente vacío los lunes / *The museum is completely empty on Mondays*

Teatro / *Theater*
El teatro cerró después de las 12 / *The theater closed after 12*

Cine / *Movie Theater*
El cine está dentro del centro comercial / *The movie theater is inside the mall*

Circo / *Circus*
El circo es lo mejor de la feria / *The circus is the best of the fair*

Parque de diversiones / *Amusement park*
El parque de diversiones es un buen lugar para celebrar mi cumpleaños / *The amusement park is a good place to celebrate my birthday*

Concierto / *Concert*
El concierto de mi banda favorita estuvo increíble / *My favorite band concert was incredible*

Discoteca / *Discotheque*
La discoteca está cerrada porque es muy temprano / *The discotheque is closed because it's too early*

Restaurante / *Restaurant*
La comida de este restaurante no es muy buena / *The food in this restaurant is not very good*

Río / *River*
El río tiene muchas piedras / *The river has many stones*

Cafetería / *Coffee shop*
La cafetería es muy linda, pero hay que ir temprano / *The coffee shop is very nice, but you have to go early.*

Casino / *Casino*
El casino está abierto todo el día, todos los días / *The casino is open all day, every day*

Montaña / *Mountain*
Me gusta esquiar en lo alto de la montaña / *I like skiing at the top of the mountain*

Pueblo / *Town*
En este pueblo hace demasiado frio en invierno / *In this town it is too cold in Winter*

Práctica de Conversación / Conversation Practice
¿Dónde está tu hotel? / *Where is your hotel?*

Mi hotel está cerca de la playa, al lado del parque de diversiones / *My hotel is near the beach, next to the amusemnt park.*

Conozco el lugar, ahí está la mejor cafetería de la ciudad / *I know the place, there is the best coffee shop in the cit.*

Sí, pero yo prefiero comer en el hotel / *Yes, but i prefer to eat at the hotel.*

Está bien, nos encontramos en el casino a las 8 p.m / *Ok, we meet at the casino at 8 p.m*

Mejor a las 6 p.m, quiero ir al museo mañana temprano / *Better at 6 p.m, I want to go to the museum early tomorrow.*

Fin del diálogo – *End of dialogue*

Actividades al aire libre / Outdoor Activities
Montar Bicicleta / *Bicycle riding*
En mi infancia, nunca monté bicicleta. / *During my childhood, I never rode a bicycle*

Correr / *Running*
Por mucho tiempo, corre fue mi actividad favorita / *Running was my favorite activity for a long time.*

Nadar / *Swimming*
Mi hermana aprendió a nadar en la piscina del hotel / *My sister learned to swim in the hotel pool.*

Escalar / *Climbing*
Escalar es mi actividad favorita / *Climbing is my favorite activity.*

Cazar / *Hunting*
No pude cazar en este bosque / *I couldn't hunt in this forest*

Picnic / *Picnic*
Hacer un picnic es una buena opción para disfrutar el día / *Having a picnic is a good option to enjoy the day.*

Pasear / *Going for a walk*
Quise caminar por las calles del pueblo, pero me duele la pierna / *I wanted to walk through the streets of the town, but my leg hurts.*

Atardecer / *Sunset*
El atardecer se ve hermoso desde la playa / *The sunset looks beautiful from the beach.*

Fogata / *Bonfire*
Tengo suficiente leña para una fogata esta noche / *I have enough wood to make a bonfire tonight.*

Fuegos artificiales / *Fireworks*
A mi perro no le gustan los fuegos artificiales / My dog doesn't like fireworks.

Festival / *festival*
Este es el festival de música más importante de Europa / *This is the most important music festival in Europe*

Navegar / *Sailing*
No puedo navegar en mi bote durante el invierno / *I can't sail on my boat during the winter*

Parrilada / *Barbecue*
Fuimos a comprar más ingredientes para la parrillada / *I went to buy more ingredients for the barbecue*

Patinar / *Skating*
A mis amigos les gusta patinar de noche / *My Friends like to skate at night*

Practica de Conversación / *Conversation practice*
Hoy es el primer día de verano, ¿Quieres hacer algo? / *Today is the first day os summer, do you want to do something?*
Yo quiero nadar en el mar / *Iwant to swim in the sea*
¡Genial! Podemos hacerlo juntos / *Great! We can do it together.*
Me gusta la idea, también podemos comprar carne y vegetales para hacer una parrillada esta noche / *I like the idea, we can also buy meat and vegetables to have a barbecue tonight.*
Si, podemos ver los fuegos artificiales desde el jardín / *Yes, we can see the fireworks from the garden.*

Fin del diálogo – *End of dialogue*

Fin del capítulo – *End of chapter*

XVIII. Pronombres Posesivos / Possessive Pronouns

Introduction: This type of pronouns is used to indicate when someone possesses something. They are placed at the end of a sentence and correspond to the English words "mine","yours", "theirs". Remember these are nouns, which means they will match gender and quantity. Always.

Possessive pronouns

Mío, mía / *Mine* (Singular masculine, singular feminine)
Aquel perro negro es mío / *That black dog is mine.*
Esta casa es mía / *This house is mine.*

Míos, mías / *Mine* (Plural masculine, plural feminine)
Estos zapatos son míos / *This shoes are mine.*
Esas fotos son mías / *Those pictures are mine.*

Tuyo, tuya / *Yours* (Singular masculine, singular feminine)
¿Éste paraguas es tuyo? / *Is this umbrella yours?*
Éstas manzanas son tuyas / *these apples are yours.*

Tuyos, tuyas / *Yours* (Plural masculine, plural feminine)
¿Son tuyos esos libros? / *Are those books yours?*
Estas pelotas son tuyas / *these balls are yours.*

Suyo, suya / *His / Hers* (Singular masculine, singular feminine)
Suyos, suyas / *His / Hers* (Plural masculine, plural feminine)

Nuestro, Nuestra / *Ours* (Singular masculine, singular feminine)
Nuestros, Nuestras / *Ours* (Plural masculine, plural feminine)
Este país es nuestro / *This country is ours*
Suyo, suya / *Theirs* (Singular masculine, singular feminine)
Suyos, suyas / *Theirs* (Plural masculine, plural feminine)
¿Estos libros son suyos? / *Are these books theirs?*

XIX. The possessive using "apostrophe « s »" in Spanish

Introduction: Compared to Spanish, English has a variety of characteristics that make it more practical or simpler. One of these could be the "'s" used to explain possession. In English, you can say "The house of my son" or "My son's house", however, in Spanish, the second way doesn't exist. Spanish will always take the "longer" path.
Vamos a los ejemplos / Let's move onto the examples

¿Este lápiz es tuyo o de José? / *Is this pencil yours or Jose's?*

¿La fiesta es en tu casa o en casa de tu mamá? / *The party is in your house or your mom's house?*

Eso no es suyo, es de mi amigo. / *That's not his, it's my friend's.*

Quick note: you could think that, following this structure, then, Spanish speakers could say "of me" or "of you", and guess what? You are half-correct. Even though the forms "of me", "of you" or "of mine / of yours" don't exist, in Spanish you can keep this structure for the rest of the pronouns.
Vamos a los ejemplos / Let's move onto the examples

¿Esa casa es de él o de ellos? / *That house is his or theirs?*

Juan es el primo de ella / *Juan is her cousin. Literally: Juan is the cousin of her.*

¿Nos vamos en mi carro o en el carro de ustedes? / *Are we going in my car or your car? Literally: ...the car of yours?*

Vocabulario / *Vocabulary*
La escuela / The school

Salón de clase , Aula de clase / *Classroom*
Este es el salón de clase de mi hijo / *This is my son's classroom*

Asignaturas , Materias / *Subjects*
¿Cuál es tu materia favorita? / *What's your favorite subject?*

Compañeros de clase / *Classmates (plural masculine form)*
Los compañeros de clase de José son muy buenos / *Jose's classmates are very good*

Pupitres / *Desks*
¿Este es pupitre es tuyo o suyo? / *This desk is yours or hers?*

Pizarra , Pizarrón / *Whiteboard*
La maestra escribe mucho en la pizarra / *The teacher writes a lot on the whiteboard*

Primaria / *Elementary school*
La hermana de Maria todavía va a la escuela primaria / *María's sister still goes to elementary school*

Secundaria / *Middle school*
Me encanta la escuela secundaria de mi primo / *I love my cousin's middle school*

Quick note: the "taking-the-long-way" structure in Spanish also happens when the adjective describes the specific characteristics such as the content, a career specialization and materials.
Vamos a continuar con los ejemplos / *Let's continue with the examples*

Maestro, Maestra / *Teacher*
Ella es la maestra de español de María / *She is Maria's Spanish teacher*
José es tu profesor de matemáticas este año / *Jose is your math teacher this year*

Clase / *Class*
¿A qué hora es la clase de arte? / *What time is the art class?*

Asignaturas / Subjects

Matemática / *Math*
Ciencia / *Science*
Física / *Physics*
Química / *Chemestry*
Biología / *Biology*
Arte / *Arts*
Educación física / *P.E*
Literatura / *Literature*

1) ¿Cuál es tu asignatura favorita? – *What's your favorite subject?*
- Creo que me gusta mucho matemática – *I think I like math a lot*
¿En serio? Bueno a mí me parece muy aburrida – *Really? Well, I think it's so boring.*

2) Maria, recuerda llevar temprano mañana a la clase de física. – *Maria, remember to get early tomorrow to physics class.*
- ¿Por qué? ¿Tenemos examen? – *Why? Do we have a test?*
Sí – *We do.*

3) Mi mama es profesora de biology, por eso soy muy bueno en esa materia – *My mom is a biology teacher, that's wht I'm so good in this subject.*

Fin del diálogo - *End of dialogue*

Objetos del salón de clase / Classroom objects

Lápiz / *Pencil*
¿Me puedes prestar un lápiz? – *Can you lend me a pencil?*

Borrador / *Eraser*
El maestro utiliza el borrador / *The teacher uses the eraser*

Marcador / *Marker*
Los marcados son de la maestra / *The markers are from the teacher*

Cuaderno / *Notebook*
Este es el cuaderno de la maestra / *This is the teacher's notebook*

Libro / *Book*
Este es un libro de ciencias / *This is a science book*

Fin del capítulo / End of chapter

XX. Los pronombres objeto directo

Introduction: an object pronoun explains who or what's being affected by a verb's action. In English, they are "me", "you", "him","her"… in sentences like "Do *me* a favor", "look at *you*", "say *it*"… All of these words are placed immediately after the action and they will always replace the person or the object. When they are directely affected by an action, they will be called direct object pronoun.

In Spanish, a "direct" action, most of the time will be a verb that is not followed by a preposition i.e. "a", "para", "de", "con", "en"… such is the case of "to eat", "to hit", "to drink", "to visit" which, in common situations, won't be followed by any preposition.

Vamos a comenzar / Let's begin

Me 7 *Me*
Él me golpeó / *He hit me*

Te / *You*
Yo te conozco / *I know you*

Lo / *Him or It (when it's replacing a masculine object)*
Tú eres la hermana de José, ¡yo lo conozco! / *Are you José's sister? I know him!*
Ayer vi un teléfono. Quiero comprarlo / *Yesterday I saw a cellphone. I want to buy it*

La / *Her or it (when replacing a feminine object)*
Necesito hablar con María, ¿puedes llamarla mañana? / *I need to talk to María, can you call her tomorrow?*
¿Conoces esta película? Debes verla / *Do you know this film? You must see it.*

Nos / *Us*
El capitán nos salvó / *The captain saved us*

Los / *You (plural)*
Wow chicos, son mis mejores amigos, los amo. – *Wow guys, you are my best Friends, I love you.*

Los, Las / *Them (masculine and feminine form)*
Mira esos pantalones, están en oferta. Tenemos que comprarlos – *Look at those pants, they are on sale. We have to buy them*
Tu cuarto está desordenado. Por favor toma todas tus cosas y ponlas en su lugar – *Your room is messy. Please take all of your stuffs and put them in their place.*

Vocabulario
Materiales / *Materials*

Bronce / *Bronze*
Alejandro vio ayer un antiguo reloj de bronce y hoy lo compró / *Yesterday, Alejandro saw an old bronze clock and today he bought it*

Plata / *Silver*
Esta es una cadena de plata 100% original. Llévala contigo ahora / *This is a 100% original silver necklace. Take it with you now.*

Oro / *Gold*
El oro es uno de los minerales más caros. ¿Lo sabías? / *Gold is one of the most expensive minerals. Did you know it?*

Diamante / *Diamond*
Mira esta espada de diamante. El gran guerro la usó para ganar todas las batallas / *Look at this diamond sowrd. The great warrios used it to win all the battles.*

Madera / *Wood*
La madera del roble es muy buena y resistente. Úsala para las puertas de tu casa / *The oak wood is very good and resistant. Use it for your house's doors*

Minerales / *Minerals*
Debajo de la superficie de la tierra hay muchos minerales. La gente cava para encontrarlos / *Beneath the earth surface, there are a lot of mineral. People dig in order to find them*

Piedra / *Stone*
Mira esta piedra, ¡está hermosa! ¡Cómprala! – *Look at this Stone, it's beautiful! Buy it!*

Plástico / *Plastic*
El plástico contamina. No lo arrojes al mar – *Plastic pollutes. Don't throw it to the sea*

Papel / *Paper*
¿Cómo haces el origami? Lo hago con papel – *How do you do origami? I do it with paper*

Metal / *Metal*
El rodio es el metal más caro del mundo – *Rodium is the most expensive metal in the world*

Hierro / *Iron*
La carne roja es buena fuente de hierro. Deberías comerla si no eres vegetariano. – *Red meat is a good source of iron. You should eat it if you are not vegetarian*

Cobre / *Copper*
El cobre es buen conductor de electricidad. Las empresas lo usan para hacer cables eléctricos – *Copper is used a good electricity conductor. Companies use it to make electric wires*

Comida III / *(Food III)*
Panqueca / *Pancake*
¿Te gustan las panquecas? Mi mamá las prepara con chocolate. / *Do you like pancakes? My mom prepares them with chocoalte*

Harina / *Flour*
¿Puedes comprarnos un poco de harina para el pastel? / *Can you buy us a bit of flour for the cake?*

Gelatina / *Jelly*
Si quieres una gelatina para la merienda, no olvides comprarla / *If you want jelly for snack, don't forget to buy it.*

Sánduche o Sandwich / *Sandwich*
Es muy difícil comer este sandwich así. ¿Lo cortas por favor? / *It's hard to eat this sándwich like this. Can you cut it please?*

Papas fritas / *Fries*
Toma las papas, córtalas y fríelas en aceite / *Take the potatos, cut them and fry them in oil*

Dulces, Golosinas / *Candies*
Me encantan los dulces, pero no los puedo comer siempre / *I love candies, but I can't always them*

Avena / *Oats*
Todas las mañanas preparo avena con miel / *Every morning I prepare oats with honey*

Tortilla / *Omelette*
Cuando la tortilla está lista, agrega queso y luego la tiene que doblar / *When the omelette is ready, add cheese and then you have to fold it*

Espinaca / *Spinach*
Me encanta la tortilla de espinaca / *I love spinach omelette*

Soya / *Soy*
Dicen que la soya es nutritiva. La tenemos que comprar / *They say soy is nutritive. We have to buy it.*

Té / *Tea*
Me gusta el té verde. Lo preparo todas las noches / *I like green tea. I prepare it every night*

Cerveza / *Beer*
¿Compraron las cervezas para la fiesta? Sí, las pusimos en la nevera / *Did you guys buy the beers for the party? Yes, we put them in the fridge*

Ice / *Hielo*
Si tienes dolor de cabeza, toma un poco de hielo y lo colocas en la frente / *If you have headache, take a bit of ice and put it on the forehead*

Interesting fact: through this chapter, you might have noticed that the object pronouns were placed sometimes before and sometimes after the verbs. This is because of a basic grammar rule for most of the pronouns. In a simple tense, a sentence with only one verb will always have the object pronoun before it. For example:
Yo la corto / *I cut it*
Tú me dices / *You tell me*
Nosotros los invitamos / *We invite them*
However, this is when it gets interesting: For sentences with two verbs or verbal periphrasis, the object pronoun in this case, can be placed *before* the first verb or *with* the second verb. Both choices are totally correct regardless the country your visiting or the person you are talking to. This means that it is always up to you to choose which one you want to use. For example:

¿Quieres comprarla? / *Do you want to buy it?*
¿La quieres comprar? / *Do yout want to buy it?*

¿Puedes invitarnos a la fiesta? / *Can you invite us to the party?*
¿Nos puedes inviter a la fiesta? / *Can you invite us to the party?*

Tengo que verlo mañana / *I have to see him tomorrow*
Lo tengo que ver mañana / *I have to see him tomorrow*

Fin del capítulo / *End of chapter*

XXI. Pronombres objeto indirecto / Indirect Object Pronoun

Introduction: The first most important thing to have in mind when focusing of the name "object pronoun" and start thinking about if it's either a direct or an indirect action, is to always remember that, basically, in Spanish, there will be only one difference between direct and indirect object. This is the pronoun *"le"* or *"les"* (in this plural form). This pronoun will replace the direct pronouns *"lo"* or *"la"* and their plural forms, for those actions considered "indirect" actions. For the rest of the pronouns, they are the same as the ones you learned before.

The second most important thing is to pay attention to the verb or action. Most of the time, an indirect veb will be linked to the preposition "to" or *"a"* in Spanish. So; give, tell, ask, take, or bring something to someone" are great common examples of indirect actions.
Continuamos / Let's continue

Me / *Me*
Él me dice algo importante / *He tells me something important*

Te / *You*
Yo te presté dinero ayer / *Yesterday, I loan you some money*

Le / *Him, her*
Ella le dije algo (a José) / *She told him something (to Jose)*
Yo le di un regalo (a mi mamá) / *I gave her a gift (to my mom)*

Nos / *Us*
El profesor nos preguntó muchas cosas / *The teacher asked us a lot of things*

Les / *You (plural)*
Chicos, les quiero pedir un favor / *Guys, I want to ask you a favor*

Les / *Them (masculine and feminine form)*
Hablé con mis amigos y les dije que pueden venir a mi fiesta / *I talked to my friends and I told them they can come to my party*

<u>Vocabulario / *Vocabulary*</u>
<u>Géneros de películas / *Movies genres.*</u>
Acción / *Action*
A mi novia no le gustan las películas de acción / *My girlfriend doesn't like action movies.*

Drama / *Drama*
El drama es un género muy comercial / *Drama is a very comercial genre.*

Comedia / *Comedy*
Estoy viendo una serie de comedia, pero no es muy buena / *I am watching a comedy series, but it's not very good.*

Documental / *Documentary film*
Están haciendo un documental sobre las playas de mi país / *They are making a documentary film about the beaches of my country.*

Animación / *Animation*
La animación de esta película es muy realista / *The animation in this movie is very realistic.*

Biografia / *Biography*
Esta serie es una biografía de Leonardo Da Vinci / *This series is a biography of Leonardo Da Vinci.*

Ciencia Ficción / *Science fiction*
Los japoneses hacen buenas películas de ciencia ficción / *The japanese make good science fiction movies.*

Artes marciales / *Martial arts*
En ese canal solo pasan películas de artes marciales / *Only martial arts movies show on that channel.*

Comedias románticas / *Romantic Comedies (Rom / Coms)*
Todas las comedias románticas me hacen llorar / *All the romantic comedies make me cry.*

Cine de Autor / *Author Cinema*
El cine de autor nos muestra otra perspectiva / *Author Cinema shows us another perspective.*

Cine Mudo / *Silent movie*
El cine mudo es ideal para mi abuelo, porque él no escucha muy bien / *Silent movies are ideal for my grandfather, because he doesn't listen very well.*

Caricaturas / *Cartoons*
Hay más de diez canales de caricaturas / *There are more than ten cartoon channels.*

Policias / *Cops*
Las series de policías y detectives son todas iguales / *The cops and detective series are all the same.*

Serie / *Series*
Me encantan las series de Netflix / *I love Netflix series*

Temporada / *Season*
Estoy esperando la nueva temporada de la serie, es muy emocionante / *I am looking forward to the new season of the series, it is very exciting.*

Práctica de Conversación / *Conversation Practice*

¿Cuál es tu película de acción favorita? / *What is your favorite action movie?*

No me gustan las películas de acción, prefiero las comedias románticas / *I don't like action movies, I prefer romantic comedies.*

También me gustan las comedias románticas, las conozco todas / *I also like romantic comedies, I know them all.*

Bueno, mañana empieza el festival de cine, ¿quieres ir conmigo? / *Well, tomorrow begins the film festival, do you want to go with me?*

Seguro, ahora tengo que irme, hay una serie que quiero ver esta noche / *Sure, now I have to go, there is a series I want to see tonight.*

Bien, adios, nos vemos mañana a las seis de la tarde en la estación del metro / *Well, bye, see you tomorrow at six o'clock in the afternoon at the subway station.*

Bien, hasta mañana / *Well, see you tomorrow.*

Fin del diálogo / *End of dialogue*

Fin del capítulo / *End of chapter*

XXII. Pronombre "Lo / La" vs Pronombre "Le" / Pronoun "Lo / La" vs Pronoun "Le"

Yo conozco un restaurante muy bueno. Yo lo conozco / *I know a very good restaurant. I know it.*

Ella dice algo a Jesus. Ella le dice algo / *She says something to Jesus. She tell him something.*

Nosotros vamos a comprar un auto. Nosotros vamos a comprarlo. *We are going to buy a car. We are going to buy it*

Tú quieres comprar un auto a tu hijo. Tu quieres comprarle un auto / *You want to buy a car to your son. You want to buy him a car*

Alejandro y Ana conocen todos los países de Latinoamérica. Alejandro y Ana los conocen todos / *Alejando and Ana know all of the latinamerican countries. Alejandro and Ana knows them all*

Ellos dan una sorpresa a su abuela. Ellos le dan un regalo / *They give their grandma a surprise. They give her a surprise*

Quick note: The pronoun "le" is always necessary when someone does something to a third person i.e. "to him", "to her", "to them". So, it is considered a small flaw in Spanish to say "Yo digo a María" instead of "Yo le digo a María" or "Tú prestas dinero a Jose" instead of "Tú le prestas dinero a Jose". Keep this always in mind.

<u>Vocabulario / *Vocabulary*</u>
<u>Etapas de la vida / *Stages of life.*</u>

Embarazo / *Pregnancy*
María está feliz con su segundo embarazo / *María is happy with her second pregnancy.*

Nacimiento / *Birth*
Mi madre no sabe la hora de su nacimiento / *My mother does not know the time of her birth.*

Edad / *Age*
Es imposible saber la edad de mi tortuga / *It is imposible to know the age of my turtle.*

Infancia-Niñez / *Childhood*
Él practica deportes desde la infancia / *He practices sports since childhood.*

Juventud / *Youth*
Hoy es el día de la juventud en Argentina / *Today is the Youth Day in Argentina.*

Adolescencia / *Adolescence*
Mi madre dice que la adolescencia es la etapa de la vida más difícil / *My mother says that adolescence is the most difficult stage of life.*

Adulto / *Adulto* - Adultez / *Adulthood*
Quiero un boleto para un niño y otro para un adulto, por favor / *I want a ticket for a child and another for an adult, please.*

Vejez / *Old age*
Quiero pasar mi vejez en una playa del Caribe / *I want to spend my old age on a Caribbean beach.*

Matrimonio / *Marriage*
Hoy es el matrimonio de mi mejorr amiga / *Today is my best friend's marriage.*

Noviazgo / *Engagement*
Ellos tienen treinta años de noviazgo / *They have thirty years of engagement.*

Novia ; Novio / *Girlfriend ; Boyfriend*
¿Sabes quién es la novia de mi hijo? Yo no la conozco. *Do you know who's my son's girlfriend. I don't know her.*
Divorcio / *Divorce*
Llamé a mi esposa y le dije que quiero el divorcio / *I called y wife and I told her that I want a divorce.*

Enfermedad / *Disease*
¿Qué enfermedad tiene mi hija?. ¿Puede salvarla? / *What disease has my daughter? Can you save her?*

Adopción / *Adoption*
La adopción es una posibilidad que estamos analizando / *Adoption is a possibility that we are analyzing.*

Muerte / *Death*
El piensa que la muerte es algo natural y no se preocupa por eso / *He thinks that death is a natural process and does not care about it.*

Práctica de Conversación / *Conversation Practice*
Abuelo, ¿Cuál es la mejor etapa de tu vida? / *Granddad, what is the best stage of life?*
Todas son buenas, pero, para mí, la juventud es la mejor / *All are good, but for me, the best is youth.*
Yo pienso que es la niñez, no quiero ser adulto, es muy duro / *I think it is childhood, I don't want to be an adult, it's very hard.*
Tienes que aprender a disfrutar todas las etapas / You have to learn to enjoy all the stages.
Tienes razón, son muchas etapas, pero solo tenemos una vida / *You are right, there are many stages, but we only have one live.*
Fin del diálogo / *End of dialogue*

XXIII. Religiones y doctrinas / Religions and doctrines.

Las religions y doctrinas son diferentes en cada cultura / *Religions and doctrines are different in each culture.*

Dios / *God*
Tu dios es diferente al mío / *Your god is different from mine.*

Diosa / *Goddess*
Los griegos creen en la diosa del conocimiento / *The greeks believe in the goddess of knowledge.*

Fe / *Faith*
Ese hombre ha perdido la fe en su equipo de béisbol / *That man has lost faith in his baseball team.*

Oración / *Prayer*
El niño está diciendo una oración antes de cenar / *The child is saying a prayer before dinner.*

Ángel / *Angel*
Hay un gran ángel en lo alto del edificio / *There is a great angel at the top of the building.*

Altar / *Altar*
El restaurante tiene un altar en la cocina / *The restaurant has an altar in the kitchen.*

Bautismo / *Baptism*
El bautismo es muy importante en su religión / *Baptism is very important in their religión.*

Iglesia / *Church*
La iglesia está a dos cuadras de aquí / *The church is two blocks from here.*

Templo / *Temple*
Este templo está hecho de madera / *This temple is made of wood.*

Creyente / *Believer*
Él es creyente desde niño / *He is a believer since he was a child.*

Pascuas / *Easter*
Estoy de vacaciones por las pascuas / *I am on vacation for Easter.*

Milagro / *Miracle*
Es un milagro encontrarte aquí / *It's a miracle to find you here.*

Evangelio / *Gospel*
No sé nada sobre el evangelio, quiero aprender un poco / *I don't know anything about the gospel, I want to learn a little.*

Cristianismo / *Christianism*
Mi abuelo está escribiendo un libro sobre el cristianismo / *My grandfather is writing a book about christianism.*

Budismo / *Buddhism*
El budismo es muy espiritual / *Buddhism is very spiritual.*

Protestante / *Protestant*
La familia de mi novio es protestante / *My boyfriend's family is Protestant.*

Ateo / *Atheist*
Ella es atea pero respeta las creencias de los demás / *She is an atheist, but she respects the beliefs of others.*

Judío / *Jewish*
Su tío es judío, vive en Tel Aviv / *Her uncle is jewish, he lives in Tel Aviv.*

Islamismo / *Islamism*
El islamismo tiene muchos años de historia / *Islam has many years of history.*

Cielo / *Heaven*
Yo creo que el cielo está en la tierra / *I believe that heaven i s on earth.*

Infierno / *Hell*
Los bomberos están apagando el infierno / *Firefighters are putting out hell.*

Pecado / Sin
Ese pecado no merece perdón / That sin does not deserve forgiveness.

Sacerdote / *Priest*
Mi hermano menor quiere ser sacerdote / *My younger brother wants to be a priest.*

Teología / *Theology*
Estoy leyendo un viejo libro de teología / *I am Reading an old theology book.*

Monja / *Nun*
Esa monja canta muy bien / *That nun sings very well.*

Práctica de Conversación / *Conversation Practice*
¿Cuál es tu opinión sobre las religiones? / *What is your opinion about religions?*
No me gusta hablar de religiones ni doctrinas / *I don't like to talk about religions or Doctrines.*

Te entiendo, yo soy estudiante de teología, por eso me interesa saber tu opinión / *I understand you, I am a theology student, so I am interested in knowing your opinion.*
Todos somos libres de elegir una religión, mis padres son cristianos y mi tío es budista / *We are all free to choose our religion , my parents are Christians and my uncle is Buddhist.*
Claro, todo se basa en respeto / *Sure, everything is based on respect.*
Estoy de acuerdo contigo / *I agree with you.*

Fin del diálogo / *End of dialogue*

Fin del capítulo / *End of chapter*

XIV. Conectores / *Connectors.*

Introduction: In Spanish like in English, Connectors are used to link words that connect parts of a text. They help to organize the ideas and sentences and provide the text with cohesion and coherence.

Conectores Aditivos / *Additive connectors.*

Además / *In addition*
Me aceptaron en la universidad y, además, me dieron una beca / *They accepted me to the university and, in addition, they gave me a scholarship.*

Aparte / *Besides*
No quiero ir al cine contigo. Aparte, no tengo dinero / *I don't want to go to the movies with you. Besides, I have no money.*

Asimismo / *Likewise*
Asimismo, los estudiantes deben presentar los certificados originales / *Likewise, students must present the original certificates.*

También / *Also*
Salí a comprar pan y, también, huevos / *I went out to buy bread and also eggs.*

Tampoco / *Neither*
No hay fruta en el supermercado, tampoco hay verdura / *There is no fruit in the supermarket, neither vegetables.*

Encima / *On top of that*
Hoy perdí el autobús. Encima, me han robado el teléfono celular / *Today I missed the bus. On top of that, my cell phone has been stolen.*

De hecho / *In fact*
Soy intolerante a la lactosa, de hecho, no puedo comer helados / *I am lactose intolerant, in fact I cannot eat ice cream.*

Por otro lado / *On The other hand*
La habitación es muy pequeña. Por otro lado, es bastante bonita / *The room is very small. On the other hand, it is quite pretty.*

Por si fuera poco / *As if that were not enough*
Me robaron la bici y, por si fuera poco, empezó a llover / *My bike was stolen and, as if that were not enough, it started to rain.*

Sobre todo / *Above all.*
Sobre todo, necesitamos financiación para sacar adelante el proyecto / *Above all, we need funding to carry the project forward.*

Conectores Adversarios / *Adversative connectors*

Al contrario / *On the contrary*
En Madrid no hace siempre calor. Al contrario, en invierno hace bastante frío / *Madrid is not always hot. on the contrary, in winter it is quite cold.*

Así y todo / *Even so*
El sueldo de Andrés es bastante alto. Así y todo, es un poco bajo para ser en la capital / *Andrés's salary is quite high. Even so, it is a bit low to be in the capital.*

En cambio / *Instead.*
Mi madre no puede venir a visitarnos, en cambio, nosotros podemos visitarla a ella / *My mother cannot come to visit us, Instead, we can go visit her.*

No obstante / *However*
El menú parece delicioso, no obstante, es muy costoso / *The menu looks delicious, however, it is very expensive.*

Por el contrario / *Conversely*
Yo soy muy bajita. Mi hermana, por el contrario, es bastante alta / *I am very short. My sister, conversely, is quite tall.*

Sin embargo / *Nevertheless*
No pude dormir nada anoche, sin embargo, me siento descansada / *I couldn't sleep at all last night, nevertheless I feel rested.*

Todo lo contrario / *Quite the opposite*
Me dijeron que la conferencia sería aburridísima. Todo lo contrario, me pareció muy interesante / *They told me that the conference would be boring. Quite the opposite, it seemed very interesting to me.*

Conectores Consecutivos / *Consecutive connectors*

Así pues / *So that*
Me compré los zapatos en tu misma talla, así pues, puedes usarlos también / *I bought the shoes in your same size, so that you can wear them too.*

Consecuentemente / *Consequently*
La nieve ha cubierto la autopista y, consecuentemente, han cerrado el tráfico.
Consiguientemente / *Snow has covered the highway and consequently they have closed traffic.*

De ese modo / *That way*

Pedí una beca al ministerio de educación. De ese modo, podré estudiar / *I applied for a scholarship to the Ministry of Education. That way, I can study.*

En consecuencia / *in consecuense*
Ha llovido mucho y, en consecuencia, las calles se han inundando / *It has rained a lot and consequently the streets have been flooded.*

Entonces / *Then*
Si no puedes venir mañana, entonces, te veré la semana que viene / *If you can't come tomorrow then I will see you next week.*

Por consiguiente / *Therefor*
El alumno ha copiado en el examen, por consiguiente, ha sido expulsado / *The student has cheated on the exam, therefor, he has been expelled.*

Por ende / *Thus*
Hemos perdido la financiación, por ende, hemos paralizado el proyecto / *We have lost funding, thus, we have paralyzed the project.*

Por esta razón / *for this reason*
Soy vegetariano, por esta razón, no como carne / *I am a vegetarian, for this reason, I do not eat meat.*

Pues / *Well*
¿No te comes la sopa? Pues la tendrás para cenar también / *Don't you eat the soup? Well, you'll have it for dinner too.*

Conectores explicativos / *Explanatory Connectors*

A saber / *Namely*
Aún debemos tomar algunas decisiones sobre el viaje; a saber: hora de salida y punto de encuentro / *We still need to make some decisions about the trip, namely: departure time and meeting point.*

Es decir / *Meaning*
La cocina es eléctrica, es decir, no es de gas / *The kitchen is electric, meaning, is not gas.*

Esto es / *That is*
El trabajador rinde estupendamente, es decir, trabaja muy bien / *The worker performs superbly, that is, he works very well.*

O sea / *I mean, in other words.*
El primer premio ha quedado desierto, o sea, nadie ha ganado / *The first prize has been deserted, un other words, nobody has won.*

Conectores concesivos / Concessive connectors

Aún así / *Still*
Me tomé un analgésico para el dolor de cabeza, aún así, me duele / *I took a pain reliever for my headache, still it hurts.*

En cualquier caso / *In any case*
En abril el tiempo es muy cambiante. En cualquier caso, yo siempre llevo un paraguas encima / *In April the weather is very changeable. In any case, I always carry an umbrella with me.*

De todas formas, de todos modos / *Anyway*
No tengo mucho tiempo, pero, de todas formas, te ayudaré / *I don't have much time, but I'll help you anyway.*

Conectores recapitulativos / Recapitulatives Connectors

A fin de cuentas / *After all*
Nos mudamos de apartamento. A fin de cuentas, el antiguo era demasiado pequeño / *We moved to another apartment. after all, the old one was too small.*

En conclusión / *In conclusion*
La empresa a aumentado los ingresos y reducido los costes. En conclusión, tiene más beneficios / *The company has increased revenues and reduced costs. In conclusion, it has more benefits.*

En definitiva / *Definitely*
El horno ya no calienta y la nevera no enfría. En definitiva, tenemos que comprar electrodomésticos nuevos / *The oven does not heat anymore and the refrigerator does not cool. Definitely, we have to buy new appliances.*

Conectores de Ordenación / *Sort connectors*

Antes que nada / *First of all*
Antes de nada, me gustaría dar las gracias a la organización por invitarme / *First of all, I would like to thank the organization for inviting me.*

Inicialmente / *Initially*
En esta casa vivimos cuatro personas. Inicialmente, éramos tres / *Four people live in this house. Initially, there were three of us.*

Para empezar / *To start with*
La receta es muy fácil. Para empezar, hay que pelar las papas / *The recipe is very easy. To start with, you have to peel the potatoes.*

Previamente / *Previously*
Pedro dimitió ayer. Previamente, había informado a sus compañeros / *Pedro resigned yesterday. Previously, he had informed her companions.*

Actualmente / *Currently*
Quiero mudarme pero, actualmente, no hay apartamentos en alquiler / *I want to move but currently there are no apartments for rent.*

En este (ese) momento / *At the (that) moment*
El ladrón salió de la joyería y, en ese momento, apareció la policía / *The thief came out of the jewelry store and, at that moment, the police appeared.*

Mientras tanto / *In the meantime*
Yo estudio, y tú, mientras tanto, sales a pasear / *I study, and you go out for a walk, in the meantime.*

De pronto, de repente / *Suddenly*
De pronto, el motor del coche se paró / *Suddenly the car's engine stopped.*

Finalmente / *Finally*
Finalmente, se deja secar el mueble doce horas / *Finally, the furniture is left to dry for twelve hours.*

Para terminar / *To finish*
Para terminar, hay que decorar el pastel con la crema / *To finish, you have to decorate the cake with the cream.*

XXV. Conjunciones / Conjunctions

Introduction: The function of the conjunction is to link two or more words or two or more sentences. The most used un Spanish are:

Ya que / *As*
Daniel es el presidente de esta compañía ya que es muy inteligente / *Daniel is the president of this company as he is very smart.*

Porque / *Because*
Espérame 5 minutos por favor porque tengo que enviar este correo / *Please wait for me 5 minutes because I have to send this email.*

Puesto que / *Since*
Puesto que sus padres hablan español, María lo aprende muy rápido / *Since her parents speak Spanish, María learns it very fast.*

Que / *Then*
Victoria es más joven que Juan / *Victoria is younger than Juan.*

Si / *If*
Si hace calor, enciende el aire acondicionado / *If it's hot, turn on the air conditioning.*

Con tal, mientras que / *As long as*
Con tal que te levantes temprano, no importa la hora que te duermas / *As long as you get up early, it doesn't matter what time you fall asleep.*

Pero / *But*
Sus palabras son muy convincentes, pero yo no confío en él / *His words are very convincing, but I don't trust him.*

O / *Or*
O nos damos prisa, o perderemos el tren / *Either we hurry, or we'll miss the train.*

A menos que / *Unless*
No iré a la fiesta de Luis mañana por la noche, a menos que tú vayas / *I'm not going to Luis's party tomorrow night, unless you go.*

Vocabulario / *Vocabulary*

Accesorios / *Accessories*

Los accesorios se venden por separado / *Acsesories are sold separately.*

Moda / *Fashion*
Los pantalones rojos no están de moda / *Red pants are not in fashion.*

Sombrero / *Hat*
Mi abuelo tiene un sombrero negro en su casa / *My grandfather has a black hat at home.*

Billetera / *Wallet*
No me gusta esa billetera, es muy pequeña / I don't like that walet, it's too small.

Reloj / *watch*
Este reloj es el favorito de mi padre / *This Watch is my father's favorite.*

Cinturón / *Belt*
El cinturón de Carlos tiene tres colores / *Carlos's Belt has three colors.*

Bufanda / *Scarf*
A Ana le gusta usar su bufanda en primavera / *Ana likes to wear her scarf in spring.*

Aretes , Zarcillos / *Earrings*
Mis aretes no son de oro / *My earrings are not gold.*

Anillo / *Ring*
Tengo un anillo muy lindo, pero no me gusta usarlo / *I have a very nice ring, but I don't like to wear it.*

Pulsera / *Bracelet*
La pulsera tiene diamantes de la India / *The bracelet has diamonds from India.*

Joyas / *Jewels*
Aquí las joyas son baratas / *Here the jewels are cheap.*

Guantes / *Gloves*
Hace mucho frio, necesito mis guantes negros / *It's so cold, I need my black gloves.*

Lentes de sol / *Sunglasses*
Mi hermana siempre usa lentes de sol / *My sister always wears sunglasses.*

Mochila / *Backpack*
Tengo la comida en mi mochila / *I have food in my backpack.*

Llavero / *Key Chain*

Este llavero es un recuerdo de París / *This Keychain is a souvenir from Paris.*

Pañuelo / *Handkerchief*
No encuentro mi pañuelo, no está en ningún lado / *I can't find my handkerchief, It's nowhere to be found.*
Gorra / *Cap*
Tengo la gorra de mi equipo de béisbol favorito / *I have the cap of my favorite baseball team.*

Práctica de Conversación / *Conversation Practice*
Ana, me encanta tu bufanda / *Ana, I love your Scarf.*
Gracias, tengo un sombrero con el mismo diseño / *Thank you, I have a hat with the same design.*
En el centro comercial hay un cinturón con esos mismos colores / *In the mall there is a belt with those same colors.*
¡Genial, vamos para allá! También quiero comprar unos lentes de sol / *Great, Let's go there, I also want to buy a pair of sunglasses.*
Ok, yo solo necesito comprar guantes para el invierno / *Ok, I just need to buy gloves for the Winter.*

Fin del diálogo / *End of dialogue*

Fin del capítulo / *End of chapter*

XXVI. Verbos esenciales / Essential verbs

Para viajar / *For travelling*

Viajar / *To travel*
Mañana viajo a Argentina / *Tomorrow I travel to Argentina*

Reservar / To book
Necesitas reservar mínimo con 15 días de anticipación / *You need to book at least 15 days in advance*

Hospedarse ; Alojarse / *To stay in a hostal or hotel*
¿En cuál hotel te hospedas? – *What hotel are you staying in?*

Llegar / *To arrive*
¿A qué hora llegas? / *What time do you arrive?*

Regresar / *To return, To come back*
Regreso mañana en la tarde / *I come back tomorrow afternoon*

Llevar / *To bring*
Recuerda siempre llevar tu pasaporte / *Remember always to bring your Passport*

En el restaurante / *In the restaurant*

Ordenar, Pedir / *To order*

Quiero ordenar una pizza, por favor / *I want to order a pizza*

Quiero pedir un café / *I want to order a coffee*

Pagar la cuenta / To pay the bill

¿Podemos pagar la cuenta con tarjeta de crédito? / *Can we pay the bill with credit card?*

Beber, Tomar / *To drink*

Yo tomo vino solamente / *I only drink wine*

Compartir / *To share*

Vamos a compartir el postre / *Let's share the dessert*

Brindar / *To toast*

Brindo por ti / *Toast to you*

Para trabajar / For working

Llamar / *To call*

Por favor, ¿puedes llamar a este cliente ahora? / *Please, can you call this client now?*

Agendar una cita / *To set an appointment*

Vamos a agendar una cita para mañana / *Let's set an appointment for tomorrow*

Cobrar / *To charge, To collect, To receive salary*

Necesito cobrar mi salario / *I need to receive my salary*

¿Cuánto me cobras por este trabajo? / *How much do you charge for this job?*

Pagar / *To pay*

Te pago 100 dólares / *I pay you 100 dollars*

Abrir / *To open*

Abrimos a las 7 / *We open at 7*

Cerrar / *To close*

Cerramos a las 8 / *We close at 8*

Despedir / *To fire*

Me despidieron de mi trabajo / *I was fired from my job*

Renunciar / *To quit*

Mañana renuncio. No me gusta el trabajo / *Tomorrow I quit. I don't like the job*

Para cocinar / For cooking

Cortar / *To cut*

Si cortas las cebollas, es más fácil / *If you cut the onions, it's easier*

Pelar / *To peel*

Ya pelé las papas / *I already peeled the potatoes*

Mezclar , Batir / *To Mix*

Tenemos que mezclar todo en un bowl / *We have to mix everything in a bowl*

Cocinar / *To cook*

¿Cuánto tiempo hay que cocinarlo? / *How long do you have to cook it?*

Hornear / *To bake*

Luego de 20 minutos tenemos que hornear el pan / *After 20 minutes, we have to bake the bread*

Freir / *To fry*

No me gusta freir las papas / *I don't like to fry the potatoes*

Para conversar / *For talking*

Decir / *To say, To tell*

Dime la verdad / *Tell me the truth*

Contar / *To tell*

¿Quieres contarme un cuento? / *Do you want to tell me a story?*

Preguntar / *To ask a question*

Quiero preguntarte algo / *I want to ask you something*

Interrumpir / *To interrupt*

Disculpa, te interrumpo un minuto / *Excuse me, I'll interrupt you for a minute*

Responder / *To answer*

Fui a tu casa y nadie respondió / *I went to your house and nobody answered*

Disculparse / *To excuse*

¿Me disculpas? / *Do you excuse me?*

Felicitar / *To congratulate*

Te felicito por tu gran trabajo / *I congratulate you for your great job*

Para festejar / *For partying*

Salir / *To go out*

¿Salimos esta noche? / *Are we going out tonight?*

Bailar / *To dance*

¿Quieres bailar conmigo? / *Do you want to dance with me?*

Tomar un taxi / *To take a taxi*

A esta hora debemos tomar un taxi / *At this time we have to take a taxi*

Divertirse / *To have fun*

¿Te estás divirtiendo? / *Are you having fun?*

Aburrirse / *To get bored*

Me estoy aburriendo / *I'm getting bored*

CONCLUSION

And... This is it! We finally arrived at the end of this amazing journey with this Language Learning Accelerator. Congratulations!

Thank you so much for using this book to learn and improve your Spanish vocabulary. We hope this book not only gave you an inmense amount of words to use on a daily basis, but also we would be glad to know that you also retained something from every introduction, quick notes and interesting facts, as well as those fantastic dialogues and short stories, all of them originally created to give you the best experience during your learning process.

We can't stop sharing all of our knowledge and we want to give you another good way you can add to keep improving your process. One of the most effective techniques, when it comes to learning, is teaching others about the topics you just learned. Doing so creates an emotive feedback which will stick that knowledge in your brain. Remember, there's no learning without emotion!

A great way of going about doing this is by reading out 1-2 chapters from the book to your friends. By going through this process, you are not only helping your friends learn the Spanish language as you do, but you will be also simultaneously teaching yourself. This creates a beautiful win-win situation that has proven to work for many, many years in our education systems and simple every day situations.

Given the extreme amount of content to learn about and comprehend through out the entirety of this book, it is best to not only read/listen to it in 20-30 minutes chunks, but also go back through each of the chapters once you have completed them to ensure you are learning the vocabulary to your full potential. This has become the most effective technique for our listeners in the past, and it continues to be the number-one way our students learn each of the languages we have successfully taught.

Thank you again from the bottom of our hearts and we wish you the best in every new learning journey you begin! Make sure to check out the rest of what Excel Language Lessons has to offer.

¡Nos vemos pronto!

The Language Library

Learn Spanish For Beginners:

30 Days of Language Lessons- Rapidly Improve Your Grammar, Conversations& Dialogue+ Short Stories& Learn 1001 Common Phrases In Your Car& While You Sleep

Table of Contents

Chapter 1 - The Spanish Alphabet: Vowels 2

Chapter 2 - The Spanish Alphabet: Consonants 5

Chapter 3 - Basic Vocabulary: Yes, No, Thanks, Please! 10

Chapter 4 - Definite Articles 14

Chapter 5 - Personal pronouns 17

Chapter 6 - Greetings 21

Chapter 7 - Numbers 28

Chapter 8 - Months and Days of the Week 32

Chapter 9 - Indefinite Articles 36

Chapter 10 - Basic Nouns 40

Chapter 11 - Basic Adjectives 43

Chapter 12 - Basic Verbs 46

Chapter 13 - The Present Tense (part I) 51

Chapter 14 - Introducing Yourself 54

Chapter 15 - The Present Tense (part II) 58

Chapter 16 - Talking about the Family 62

Chapter 17 - The Present Tense (part III) 65

Chapter 18 - Talking about Work 68

Chapter 19 - Negative Sentences 73

Chapter 20 - Forming Questions (part I) 76

Chapter 21 - Formal and Informal Speech 79

Chapter 22 - Forming Questions (part II) 83

Chapter 23 - Telling the Time 86

Chapter 24 - Adverbs 90

Chapter 25 - Present continuous 92

Chapter 26 - Prepositions (part I) 95

Chapter 27 - Food 98

Chapter 28 - Travelling (part I) 100

Chapter 29 - Prepositions (part II) 103

Chapter 30 - Travelling (Part II) 107

Chapter 1 - The Spanish Alphabet: Vowels

The Spanish alphabet is *very* similar to the English alphabet. But here, of course, we'll focus on the differences!

The Spanish alphabet has 27 letters: 22 consonants and 5 vowels. The vowels are the same as in English: *A, E, I, O* and *U*. But, unlike in English, in Spanish these vowels are *always pronounced in the same way*.

Letter *A* is always pronounced *ah*. We find it in words such as *amar* (to love), *alfabeto* (alphabet) and *manzana* (apple).

Letter *E* is always pronounced *eh*. We can see this vowel in *estrella* (star), *espejo* (mirror) and *elegir* (to choose).

Letter *I* is always pronounced *ee*. We see it in words such as *idioma* (language), *imitar* (imitate) and *invierno* (winter).

Letter *O* is always pronounced *oh*. We can find this letter in *oso* (bear), *hongo* (mushroom) and *oler* (to smell).

Letter *U* is always pronounced *oo*. We can see this vowel in *sumar* (to add), *luz* (light) and *pluma* (feather).

The pronunciation of Spanish vowels is easy, because it never changes.

Now, practice the Spanish vowels with these 50 example sentences!

For now, don't focus on the meaning of the words, simply focus on the pronunciation.

Letra *a* - Letter *a*

La mamá canta - The mom sings

Ana es mi amiga - Ana is my friend

La sala está llena - The room is full

Álvaro ama las bananas - Álvaro loves bananas

Las abejas trabajan - The bees work

Ellas lavan las sábanas - They wash the bedsheets.

La gata salta - The cat jumps

La abogada habla - The lawyer speaks

Las papas están saladas - The potatoes are salty

La banda de jazz ensaya - The jazz band is rehearsing

Letra *e* - Letter *e*

El elefante es enorme - The elephant is huge

Ese traje es muy elegante - That suit is very elegant

Ernesto enciende el fuego - Ernesto starts the fire

Este empleo me interesa - I am interested in this job

El enfermero viene temprano - The nurse comes early

El cementerio está embrujado - The cemetery is haunted

Siempre llueve en Ecuador - It always rains in Ecuador

Hay veinte nueces en el estante - There are twenty walnuts on the shelf

El vidente me lee la mente - The psychic reads my mind

El tren no se detiene en este andén - The train does not stop on this platform

Letra *i* - Letter *i*

Isabel entiende inglés - Isabel understands English

Mi tía es muy inteligente - My aunt is very smart

Iván viaja a la India - Ivan is travelling to India

El gobierno invierte en infraestructura - The government invests in infrastructure

Un rayo ilumina el cielo - A lightning lights up the sky

Ignacio siempre imagina cosas - Ignacio is always imagining things

El ingeniero diseña un rascacielos - The engineer designs a skyscraper

El instituto cierra en el invierno - The institute closes during the winter

La chica inglesa tiene lindas ideas - The English girl has nice ideas

Irina investiga sobre la historia italiana en internet - Irina investigates Italian history on the internet

Letra *o* - Letter *o*

Oscar tiene un ojo rojo - Oscar has a red eye

Los hongos están en el horno - The mushrooms are in the oven

El oso vive solo en el bosque - The bear lives alone in the forest

Este coche no es ecológico - This car is not environmentally friendly

Osvaldo no está del todo loco - Osvaldo is not completely crazy

El dueño del bar ofrece a los comensales jugo de coco - The bar owner offers coconut juice to the clients

La doctora Ortiz odia la comida con orégano - Doctor Ortiz hates oregano in her food

El oficial de policía observa con atención la grabación del robo - The police officer carefully observes the recording of the robbery

Rocco es en extremo organizado - Rocco is extremely organized

Yo compro obsequios a menudo - I frequently buy presents

Letra *u* - Letter *u*

Las uvas son dulces - Grapes are sweet

Úrsula toca el ukelele los lunes - Úrsula plays the ukulele on Mondays

Uma pinta sus uñas de color azul - Uma paints her nails blue

El unicornio susurra - The unicorn whispers

El submarino se hunde - The submarine sinks

El suelo está sucio - The floor is dirty

Humberto cumple años un jueves - Humberto's birthday is on a Thursday

Susana es una mujer uruguaya - Susana is a Uruguayan woman

El alumno usa su uniforme - The student wears his uniform

La música de Venezuela es única - Venezuela's music is unique

Chapter 2 - The Spanish Alphabet: Consonants

The Spanish alphabet has 22 consonants: one more than the English alphabet.

This mysterious additional consonant is… letter Ñ.

Letter Ñ looks like an N with a moustache or a funny little hat, and it sits between the *N* and the *O* in the Spanish alphabet. It is pronounced *nee*, and you can find it in words like *año* (year) or *mañana* (tomorrow).

And what about the other consonants?

Letters F, M, N and S are basically pronounced just like their English equivalents. The same can be said of K, W and X. However, these three letters are rare and don't come up very frequently in Spanish.

The Spanish consonants B, D, P and T are very similar to the English ones, but a bit softer: as in *beso* (kiss), *duda* (doubt), *pato* (duck) and *taco* (heel).

The Spanish V is very similar to the Spanish B, so it's a softer English B.

Letter C has three different sounds. When followed by E or I, it's pronounced like an S, as in *cisne* (swan) or *trece* (thirteen). When followed by H, is the same as the CH combination in English, as in *chocolate*. All of the other times, it's pronounced like the English K, as in *casa* (house) or *cosa* (thing). When two Cs are placed together, they sound just like in English: for example, *acceso* means *access*.

Letter J in Spanish sounds like a stronger English H in words like 'ham'. For example: *jalapeño*.

Letter G has two pronunciations. The soft one is similar to the English G in 'game'. It appears when G is followed by consonants, A, O or U: *gato* (cat) or *guante* (glove) are some examples).

The hard G appears when it is followed by E or I. It sounds like the Spanish J. To have a soft G sound with these two vowels, you need to put a silent U between them, like in *guitarra* (guitar). However, if that U has dieresis (Ü), it means it has to be pronounced, like in *pingüino* (penguin).

H is always silent, except when preceded by a C. *Hielo* (ice) and *humano* (human) are some examples.

Regarding letter L, when you see just one, you don't need to worry: it's pronounced just like in English. However, when there are two Ls, the pronunciation depends on the country. The double L can be pronounced like the English Y in 'yes', like a soft English J, or like the English SH combination.

The pronunciation of letter Q is special, but easy to learn. It only appears in QUE and QUI combinations, where the U is silent, so the pronunciation is *ke* and *ki*. Some examples are *queso* (cheese) and *aquí* (here).

The famous "rolling R" is hard to learn for some people! But it takes only practice! Letter R has this hard sound when it is placed at the beginning of the word, like *ratón* (mouse), or when there are two Rs, as in *perro* (dog). In all other cases, the R is pronounced like the American English pronunciation of the R in 'water', as in *cara* (face).

Letter Y has two pronunciations: when it is at the end of the word or by itself, it's like a Spanish I (pronounced *ee*); when not, it's like the Spanish LL, so it depends on the country.

In Latin America, letter Z sounds just like an S. However, in Spain it sounds like the English TH in 'Thursday'.

Now, practice your Spanish consonants with these 50 sentences:

Letra *b* - Letter *b*

Brenda baja a la biblioteca - Brenda goes down to the library

La bicicleta blanca brilla - The white bicycle shines

Letra *c* - Letter *c*

Camilo cubre la cama - Camilo covers the bed

La cantante cruza la calle - The singer crosses the street

César cena cerdo con cebollas - César eats pork with onions for dinner

Cacho mancha la colcha con chocolate - Cacho stains the quilt with chocolate

La traducción es accesible - The translation is accessible

Letra *d* - Letter *d*

Daniel dona dinero - Daniel donates money

La doctora da su diagnostico - The doctor provides her diagnosis

Letra *f* - Letter *f*

Félix es famoso - Felix is famous

Fiona ofrece un frasco de frambuesas - Fiona offers a raspberry jar

Letra *g* - Letter *g*

A Gustavo le gustan los gatos - Gustavo likes cats

La guitarra guía el tango - The guitar guides the tango

El gigante es generoso - The giant is generous

Había pingüinos en la antigüedad - There were penguins in ancient times

Letter *h* - Letter *h*

El vehículo va hacia el hospital - The vehicle goes to the hospital

El muchacho escucha la charla - The boy listens to the talk

Letra *j* - Letter *j*

Jorge pasó su juventud en Jamaica - Jorge spent his youth in Jamaica

La jardinera hace jugo - The gardener makes juice

Letra *k* - Letter *k*

El koala no come kiwis - The koala does not eat kiwis

Karen toca el ukelele - Karen plays the ukelele

Letra *l* - Letter *l*

El león limpia su melena - The lions cleans his mane

La luna ilumina el lugar - The moon lights up the place

La lluvia apaga las llamas - The rain puts out the flames

La caballería llega a la batalla - The cavalry arrives to the battle

Letra *m* - Letter *m*

Manuel miente sin miedo - Manuel lies without fear

Los monos miran el mar - The monkeys look at the see

Letra *n* - Letter *n*

Natalia navega de noche - Natalia sails at night

Los novios no conocen la nieve - The couple doesn't know the snow

Letra *ñ* - Letter *ñ*

Iñaki cumple años mañana - Iñaki's birthday is tomorrow

Los niños miran al ñandú - The children look at the rhea

Letra *p* - Letter *p*

Pablo pide un plato de pasta - Pablo orders a plate of pasta

La policía patrulla el pueblo - The police patrols the town

Letra q - Letter q

Quique quiere queso - Quique wants cheese

La arquitecta está tranquila - The architect is calm

Letra r - Letter r

El perro rompe la ropa - The dog tears off the clothes

Romina corre rápido - Romina runs fast

Martina espera en el teatro - Martina waits in the theatre

El camarero llega temprano - The waiter arrives early

Letra s - Letter s

Susana sabe silbar - Susana knows how to whistle

Las serpientes son salvajes - Snakes are wild

Letra t - Letter t

Tomás tiene tres tomates - Tomás has three tomatoes

La tierra tiembla en un terremoto - The earth shakes in an earthquake

Letra v - Letter v

Valentina vuelve a Valencia - Valentina goes back to Valencia

El veterinario es vegetariano - The veterinarian is a vegetarian

Letra w - Letter w

Walter viaja a Taiwán - Walter travels to Taiwan

Letra x - Letter x

El taxista toca el saxofón - The cab driver plays the sax

Letra y - Letter y

Yolanda hace yoga - Yolanda does yoga

Hoy estoy cansado - Today I am tired

Letra z - Letter z

El zapatero caza zorros - The shoemaker hunts foxes

Chapter 3 - Basic Vocabulary: Yes, No, Thanks, Please!

Now, let's learn some basic vocabulary!

First of all, in any interaction with a Spanish speaker, you will need to know how to say *yes* and *no*. Yes in Spanish is *sí*. And no is *no*.

Other words and phrases to express agreement, disagreement and doubt are *por supuesto* (of course) and *claro* (sure); *tal vez* or *quizá* (both meaning maybe, perhaps); and *no lo sé* (I don't know). If you are very sure about something, you can also say *claro que sí* (of course!) and *claro que no* (of course not!).

Now, some basic politeness. When asking for something, we say *por favor* (please), *gracias* (thanks, thank you), *muchas gracias* (thanks a lot), *de nada* and *no hay por qué* (both meaning 'you are welcome').

Other useful phrases in a polite exchange are: *¿qué desea?* (what would you like?), *me gustaría* (I would like), *quiero* (I want), *¿es posible?* (is it possible?).

To get someone's attention, we say *disculpe* (excuse me). To apologize, we say *perdón* or *lo siento* (I'm sorry). To ask for permission to do something or to walk past someone, we say *con permiso* (may I?).

Finally, to say how we feel, we can say *bien* (well), *mal* (badly) and *más o menos* (so-so).

Find some of these words and many more in the following short story!

No, gracias - No, thanks

Un hombre entra en la tienda de mascotas. Lucía lo mira: el hombre es alto y está bien vestido. Tiene un traje negro, corbata y sombrero.

A man walks into the pet store. Lucia looks at him: the man is tall and well dressed. He has a black suit, a tie and hat.

—Buenos días —dice el hombre.

"Good morning," says the man.

—Buenos días —dice Lucía—. ¿Puedo ayudarlo?

"Good morning," says Lucia. "Can I help you?"

—Sí, muchas gracias —responde el hombre—. Quiero una mascota.

"Yes, thank you very much," the man replies. "I want a pet."

—Muy bien —responde Lucía—. ¡Este es el lugar indicado! Aquí tenemos todo tipo de mascotas. ¿Qué tiene en mente?

"Very well," Lucia replies. "This is the right place for that! We have all kinds of pets here. What do you have in mind?"

—No lo sé —dice el hombre—. Vivo solo, y me gustaría tener compañía. Pero no sé qué animal elegir.

"I don't know," says the man. "I live alone, and I would like some company. But I don't know which animal to choose."

—Tal vez un gato —propone Lucía—. A mucha gente le gustan los gatos.

"Maybe a cat," Lucia proposes. "Many people like cats."

—No, gracias —dice el hombre—. Los gatos me dan alergia.

"No thanks," says the man. "Cats give me allergies."

—Mmm… Puede ser un perro —dice Lucía—. Aquí tenemos tres hermosos cachorros. Son una excelente compañía.

"Mmm… It could be a dog," says Lucia. "Here we have three beautiful puppies. They are an excellent company."

—No, gracias —dice el hombre—. Me gustaría un animal sin tanto pelo, por favor. No quiero tener el traje lleno de pelo. La limpieza es muy importante para mí.

"No thanks," says the man. "I would like an animal without so much fur, please. I don't want my suit to be covered in dog hair. Cleanliness is very important to me."

Lucía escucha piensa. ¡No es fácil encontrar una mascota sin pelo! Finalmente, después de unos segundos, tiene una idea.

Lucia thinks. A hairless pet is not easy to find! Finally, after a few seconds, she has an idea.

—¿Quizás un pájaro? —dice Lucía—. Es una mascota original. Aquí tenemos un loro doméstico. Es colorido, amigable, ¡aprende hasta cien palabras! Y puede posarse sobre su hombro… ¡Como un pirata!

"Maybe a bird?" Lucia says. "It is an original pet. Here we have a domestic parrot. It's colorful, friendly, it can learn up to a hundred words! And it can perch on your shoulder ... Like a pirate!"

—¡No, gracias! —dice el hombre—. Me gustaría un animal más silencioso, por favor. No quiero escuchar a un pájaro que habla todo el día. Yo paso mucho tiempo en mi casa, y necesito silencio para estar cómodo.

"No, thanks!" says the man. "I would like a quieter animal, please. I don't want to listen to a bird talking all day. I spend a lot of time at home, and I need silence to be comfortable."

Lucía piensa. Un animal sin pelo… y silencioso… No hay demasiados. Por suerte, su tienda es grande y tiene muchas opciones. Enseguida tiene una nueva idea.

Lucia thinks. A hairless… and silent animal… There aren't too many. Luckily, her store is large and she has many options. Right away she has a new idea.

—Entonces, puedo ofrecerle un pez —dice Lucía—. Es un animal absolutamente silencioso. Y no tiene pelo. Pasa todo su tiempo bajo el agua; es muy limpio. Aquí tenemos muchos peces tropicales, de todos los colores.

"Then I can offer you a fish," Lucia says. "It is an absolutely silent animal. And it has no hair. It spends all its time underwater; it is very clean. We have lots of tropical fish here, of every color."

—No, gracias —dice el hombre—. No quiero tener que limpiar una pecera. Parece mucho trabajo y yo estoy muy ocupado. No tengo tiempo para eso.

"No thanks," says the man. "I don't want to have to clean a fish tank. It seems like a lot of work and I am very busy. I do not have time for that."

—Sí, es verdad, debe limpiar la pecera con frecuencia… —responde Lucía.

"Yes, it's true, you would have to clean the fish tank frequently…" Lucia replies.

Durante un rato, Lucía mira todos los animales de su tienda. ¿Un hámster? No, muy peludo. ¿Un gato esfinge? Esos no tienen pelo… Pero son ruidosos, y requieren muchos más cuidados que un pez. ¿Una serpiente? No, ella no vende reptiles.

For a while, Lucia looks at all the animals in her store. A hamster? No, very hairy. A sphinx cat? Those do not have hair … But they are noisy, and require much more care than a fish. A snake? No, she does not sell reptiles.

Entonces ¡se le ocurre una nueva idea! Lucía va al sector de decoración y busca.

Then, Lucia comes up with a new idea! She goes to the decoration sector and looks for something.

Vuelve al mostrador con una pesada roca en su mano. Es un cristal azul brillante y luminoso, con pequeñas manchas negras y rosas. ¡Una piedra hermosa!

She returns to the counter with a heavy rock in her hand. It is a bright and shiny blue crystal, with small black and pink spots. A beautiful stone!

—¿Qué le parece esta roca? —pregunta Lucía—. No hace ruido, no tiene pelo y no requiere ningún trabajo. Además, ¡ni siquiera tiene que alimentarla!

"How about this rock?" Lucia asks. "It is quiet, hairless, and requires no work. Plus, you don't even have to feed it!"

—¡Es perfecta! —exclama el hombre—. ¡Justo lo que necesito! Muchas gracias, señorita.

"It's perfect!" the man exclaims. "Just what I need! Thank you very much, Miss."

—De nada —responde Lucía—. Un placer.

"You're welcome," Lucia replies. "My pleasure."

Chapter 4 - Definite Articles

English has only one definite article: *the*. Listen to this example sentence: *The house was beautiful, but the floor was dirty. The doors were open and the dogs were inside.*

In Spanish those four 'the' are four different words: *La casa era hermosa, pero el piso estaba sucio. Las puertas estaban abiertas, y los perros estaban adentro.*

This is because all nouns in Spanish have a gender: they are either feminine or masculine. For feminine nouns, we use *la*, as in *la casa* (the house). For masculine nouns, we use *el*, as in *el piso* (the floor).

The definite articles also express if we're talking about a single or a plural noun. That is why we say *las* for feminine plural nouns, as in *las puertas* (the doors) and *los* for masculine plural nouns, as in *los perros* (the dogs).

Simple enough, right? Yes, but let's complicate things a little bit…

First of all, note that the definite article for masculine singular nouns (*el*) sounds the same as personal pronoun *él* (he). We will learn this and other personal pronouns in the next lesson, so there's no need to worry about this yet.

Now, to really make things a little bit more complicated, note that when the definite article is preceded by the prepositions *a* and *de*, they form contractions: *a* plus *el* becomes *al* (meaning *to the*); *de* plus *el* becomes *del* (meaning *from the*). Some examples are *Fui al cine* (I went to the cinema) and *Debajo del árbol* (under the tree). We will deal with prepositions later on. For now, just remember the combinations *del* and *al*.

Another thing you need to know about the definite article is that there are some feminine nouns that use the masculine *el* article. These are the ones that start with a stressed A or HA. That's why we say *el agua* (the water), for example, even though it is a feminine noun.

Last but not least, we have neuter article *lo*. *Lo* is used before adjectives and adverbs instead of nouns.

Now, practice the Spanish definite articles with these 50 example sentences:

La - Single, feminine

La vaca vive en la granja - The cow lives in the farm

La abogada llega a la casa - The lawyer arrives to the house

La respuesta correcta es la número 3 - The correct answer is number 3

La boxeadora gana la pelea - The boxer wins the fight

La nueva corbata es muy elegante - The new tie is very elegant

La policía trabaja en la noche - The police works at night

La cocinera prepara la salsa - The cook prepares the gravy

La bailarina ama a los animales - The dancer loves animals

La entrenadora prefiere los deportes de equipo - The trainer prefers team sports

La profesora conduce por la carretera - The professor drives on the road

La revista explica el tema - The magazine explains the issue

La doctora recibe a los pacientes - The doctor welcomes the patients

Ricardo toca la guitarra de la madre - Ricardo plays his mother's guitar

El - Single, masculine

El toro camina por el bosque - The bull walks through the woods

El piloto maneja el avión - The pilot drives the plane

Luciana tiene el siguiente turno - Luciana has the next turn

El portero odia los lunes - The doorman hates Mondays

El extraño golpea la puerta - The stranger knocks on the door

El secreto está a la vista - The secret is at plain sight

El cantante ensaya por las mañanas - The singer rehearses in the morning

El muchacho baja en la próxima estación - The boy gets down on the next station

El hijo recibe la buena noticia - The son receives the good news

El timbre de la casa no funciona - The doorbell of the house doesn't work

El maestro duerme en la sala de descanso - The teacher sleeps in the break room

El turismo es importante en la región - Tourism is important in the region

Las - Plural, feminine

Las puertas están abiertas - The doors are open

Las hermanas están en las habitaciones de arriba - The sisters are in the upstairs bedrooms

Las abejas construyen la colmena - The bees build the hive

María ama la playa - María loves the beach

Las hierbas aromáticas están en la otra sección - Aromatic herbs are in the other section

Las sillas están en el sótano - The chairs are in the basement

Los - Plural, masculine

Los perros conocen el edificio - The dogs know the building

Los ingenieros trabajan en el problema - The engineers work on the problem

Los candidatos fueron elegidos - The candidates were chosen

Los primos vuelven de las vacaciones - The cousins come back from the holidays

Los perros y los gatos son mascotas - Cats and dogs are pets

Pedro tiene tatuajes en las piernas y en los brazos - Pedro has tattoos in his legs and arms

Lo - Neutral, singular

Una dieta balanceada es lo mejor para la salud - A balanced diet is the best for your health

Lo único que quiero es un buen trabajo - The only thing I want is a good job

Caro es lo contrario de barato - Expensive is the opposite of cheap

No hablemos de lo sucedido - Let's not talk about what happened

¡Tus clases son lo mejor! - Your lessons are the best!

Los libros de la escuela son lo peor - School books are the worst

Contracciones - Contractions

El camarero juega al fútbol - The waiter plays football

Tokio es la ciudad más grande del mundo - Tokyo is the biggest city in the world

El gato huye del perro - The cat runs away from the dog

Lucas usa el reloj del abuelo - Lucas wears his grandfather's watch

La casa está en lo alto del monte - The house is on the top of the hill

La tarde es la mejor hora del día - The afternoon is the best time of day

Sofía pasea al perro del vecino - Sofía walks the neighbour's dog

Chapter 5 - Personal pronouns

In Spanish, the first person singular pronoun is *yo*, equivalent to the English 'I'.

When we want to address the person we are talking to, 'you', things get a bit more complicated. Spanish has three words for singular 'you': *usted, tú* and *vos*. They are used to refer both to women and men, and their usage depends on the context and the country.

Tú is used in informal contexts in Spain and most Latin American countries.

Usted is used in formal contexts in all Spanish-speaking countries.

Finally, *vos* is used in informal contexts in Argentina, Uruguay, Paraguay, most of continental Central America, some areas of Colombia and other small regions of Latin America.

The third person singular pronouns (in English, 'she' and 'he') are *ella* and *él*.

Moving forward to plural pronouns, for 'we' we have two words instead of one, a feminine and a masculine word: *nosotras* is used for all-female groups, and *nosotros*, for male or mixed groups.

For the plural 'you', just as it happened with the singular 'you', we also have some variations. In Latin America, we use *ustedes*; in Spain, we use *vosotras* (for all-female groups) and *vosotros* (for male or mixed groups).

For the plural forms (equivalent to 'they'), we have *ellas* (for all-female groups) and *ellos* (for male or mixed groups).

Now, let's practice the personal pronouns with these 50 example sentences:

Yo - I

Yo vivo en una casa - I live in a house

Yo tengo frío - I am cold

Yo amo la comida mexicana - I love mexican food

Yo juego al fútbol los domingos - I play football on Sundays

Tú - You (informal - in Spain, México and other countries)

Tú eres una persona muy agradable - You are a very nice person

Tú tienes un coche nuevo - You have a new car

Tú tocas la guitarra - You play the guitar

Tú viajas todos los veranos - You travel every summer

Vos - You (informal - in Argentina, Uruguay and other countries)

Vos sos la mejor jugadora - You are the best player

Vos tenés algo entre los dientes - You have something between your teeth

Vos comés demasiado rápido - You eat too quickly

Vos mentís todo el tiempo - You lie all the time

Usted - You (formal, in every Spanish-speaking country)

Usted es un modelo a seguir - You are a role model

Usted parece mucho más joven - You look much younger

Usted puede solucionar este problema - You can solve this problem

Usted no piensa en el futuro - You don't think about the future

Él - He

Él es el nuevo vecino - He is the new neighbour

Él estudia Física en la universidad - He studies Physics at university

Él riega las plantas - He waters the plants

Él no cree en los fantasmas - He doesn't believe in ghosts

Ella - She

Ella escribe en un periódico importante - She writes for an important newspaper

Ella vive en el último piso - She lives in the last floor

Ella tiene miedo a la oscuridad - She is afraid of the dark

Ella compra fruta orgánica - She buys organic fruit

Nosotros - We (masculine)

Nosotros somos el mejor equipo - We are the best team

Nosotros solucionamos todo tipo de problemas - We solve every kind of problem

Nosotros tenemos un plan - We have a plan

Nosotros no conocemos Ibiza - We don't know Ibiza

Nosotras - We (feminine)

Nosotras estamos preparadas para todo - We are ready for everything

Nosotras somos especialistas en Historia Latinoamericana - We are specialists in Latin American History

Nosotras tenemos hambre - We are hungry

Nosotras queremos adoptar un gato - We want to adopt a cat

Vosotros - Plural you (in Spain, masculine)

Vosotros sois el mejor grupo - You are the best group

¿Vosotros queréis un nuevo trabajo? - Do you want a new job?

Vosotros no sabéis nada - You know nothing

Vosotras - You (in Spain, feminine)

Vosotras estáis muy informadas - You are very well informed

Vosotras viajáis en los asientos del fondo - You travel in the back seats

¿Vosotras tenéis reloj? - ¿Do you have a watch?

Ustedes - You (in Latin America)

Ustedes son los nuevos empleados - You are the new employees

Ustedes tienen la mejor casa del barrio - You have the best house in the neighborhood

Ustedes están cansadas de tanto viajar - You are tired from all the travelling

Ustedes no escuchan con atención - You don't listen carefully

Ellos - They (masculine)

Ellos son estrellas de cine - They are movie stars

Ellos coleccionan monedas y estampillas - They collect coins and stamps

Ellos tienen una inmensa biblioteca - They have a huge library

Ellos no encuentran las llaves - They can't find their keys

***Ellas* - They**

Ellas son muy profesionales - They are very professional

Ellas duermen mucho - They sleep a lot

Ellas sueñan con ganar un Mundial - They dream of winning a World Cup

Ellas tienen un jardín - They have a garden

Chapter 6 - Greetings

Want to travel to Spain or Latin American and meet new people? Then you need to learn some basic greetings!

When you meet someone, you can say:

Hola (hi, hello)

Buen día (good day)

Buenos días (good morning)

Buenas tardes (good afternoon)

Buenas noches (good evening, good night)

Mucho gusto, *un gusto* (nice to meet you)

Es un placer conocerlo ('it's nice to meet you', when you are addressing a man, formal)

Es un placer conocerla ('it's nice to meet you', when you are addressing a woman, formal)

Es un placer conocerte ('it's nice to meet you', informal)

If you want to ask the other person how they are feeling, you can use one of the following:

¿Qué tal? (¿what's up?', informal)

¿Cómo está usted? ('how are you?', formal)

¿Cómo estás? ('how are you?', informal)

¿Cómo están? ('how are you?', for a group of people in Latin America)

¿Cómo estáis? ('how are you?', for a group of people in Spain)

If someone asks you how you are, you can answer with these phrases:

Bien, gracias (good, thanks)

Bien, ¿y tú? ('good, and you?'. Remember to use *tú*, *vos* or *usted*, depending on the context)

Todo bien (all good)

Muy bien (very good)

No muy bien (not so well)

Mal (bad)

Muy mal (very bad)

To say goodbye, you can say:

Hasta luego (see you later)

Nos vemos luego (I'll see you later)

Hasta pronto (see you soon)

Chau (bye)

Adiós (goodbye)

¡No hay excepciones! - No exceptions!

Ezequiel Martínez llega al enorme edificio del Ministerio de Transporte. Mira la hora, son las nueve en punto. Cruza la puerta y saluda al recepcionista:

Ezequiel Martínez arrives at the huge building of the Ministry of Transportation. He looks at the time; it's nine o'clock. He walks through the door and greets the receptionist:

—Hola —dice Ezequiel.

"Hi," Ezequiel says.

—Buenos días —responde el recepcionista—. ¿Qué desea?

"Good morning," says the receptionist. "How can I help you?"

—Mi nombre es Ezequiel Martínez. Busco la oficina de licencias de conducir.

"My name is Ezequiel Martínez. I'm looking for the driver license office."

—Un gusto, Ezequiel. ¿Tiene un número? —responde el recepcionista.

"Nice to meet you, Ezequiel. Do you have a number?" the receptionist replies.

—No, pero… —dice Ezequiel.

"No, but…" Ezequiel says.

—No puede ir a la oficina de licencias de conducir sin un número. ¡No hay excepciones!

"You can't go to the driver license office without a number. No exceptions!"

—Bueno, ¿dónde consigo un número? —pregunta Ezequiel.

"Well, where do I get a number?" Ezequiel asks.

—En la oficina 32, en el tercer piso —dice el recepcionista.
"In Office 32, on the third floor," says the receptionist.

—Bueno. Muchas gracias —dice Ezequiel, preocupado. Mira la hora su reloj—. Allí iré. Hasta luego.
"Okay. Thank you very much," says Ezequiel, concerned. He looks at the time on his wristwatch. "I'll go there. See you later."

—Chau —le dice el recepcionista.
"Bye," says the receptionist.

Ezequiel, entonces, se sube al ascensor y va hasta el tercer piso. Luego, busca la oficina 32. Frente a la puerta de la oficina, hay una larga fila. Ezequiel va hasta la puerta, pero cuando está entrando, un hombre lo detiene.

Ezequiel then gets on the elevator and goes to the third floor. Then, he looks for office 32. In front of the office door, there is a long line of people. Ezequiel goes to the door, but when he is entering the office, a man stops him.

—Buen día, señor, ¿a dónde va? —le dice el hombre.
"Good morning, sir, where are you going?" the man says.
—Buenos días —dice Ezequiel—. Tengo que ir a la oficina de licencias de conducir…
"Good morning," Ezequiel says. I have to go to the driver license office …

—Necesita un número para eso —dice el hombre.
"You need a number for that," the man says.

—Lo sé, por eso estoy aquí —dice Ezequiel.
"I know, that's why I'm here," Ezequiel says.

—Para que le den un número, necesita hacer la fila —dice el hombre, señalando la larga fila de personas que esperan junto a la puerta.
"To get a number, you need to line up," the man says, pointing to the long line of people waiting by the door.
—Pero… —dice Ezequiel.

"But..." Ezequiel says.

—¡No hay excepciones! —dice el hombre—. Debe hacer la fila.

"No exceptions!" says the man. "You must wait in line."

—Vale, gracias —dice Ezequiel, mirando la hora.

"Okay, thanks," Ezequiel says, looking at the time.

Camina hasta el final de la fila, y ahí espera. La fila tarda mucho en avanzar. Veinte minutos después, entra en la oficina.

He walks to the end of the line, and there he waits. The line takes a long time to move forward. Twenty minutes later, he walks into the office.

—¡Siguiente! —grita una mujer detrás de un escritorio. Ezequiel camina hasta ella.

"Next!" shouts a woman behind a desk. Ezequiel walks up to her.

—Hola, ¿cómo está? —dice él.

"Hi how are you?" he says

—¿A qué oficina tiene que ir? —pregunta la mujer, sin saludarlo.

"To which office do you have to go?" the woman asks, without greeting him.

—A la oficina de licencias de conducir —dice Ezequiel, algo molesto.

"To the driver license office," Ezequiel says, somewhat annoyed.

—¿Tiene su documento? —pregunta la mujer.

"Do you have your ID?" the woman asks.

—Sí, pero... —dice Ezequiel.

"Yes, but ..." Ezequiel says.

—Deme su documento, ¡no hay excepciones! —grita la mujer.

"Give me your ID, no exceptions!" the woman yells.

—Bien, tenga, aquí está —dice Ezequiel.

"Okay, here it is," Ezequiel says.

—Gracias —dice la mujer, agarrando su cédula de identidad.

"Thank you," the woman says, grabbing his identity card.

Entonces, aprieta unos botones en su teclado y sale un papel de una pequeña impresora. La mujer toma el papel y se lo da a Ezequiel junto con su documento.

Then, she presses a few buttons on her keyboard and a piece of paper comes out of a small printer. The woman takes the paper and gives it to Ezequiel along with his ID.

—Oficina 78, séptimo piso —le dice.

"Office 78, seventh floor," she tells him.

—Vale, adiós, muchas gracias —dice él.

"Okay, bye, thank you very much," he says.

—¡Siguiente! —grita ella.

"Next!" she yells.

Ezequiel mira el papel, tiene un gran número 12 impreso. Sale de la oficina y va hasta el ascensor. Va hasta el séptimo piso. Allí, busca la oficina 78. Dentro de la oficina, hay mucha gente sentada, esperando. Hay dos escritorios. Uno está vacío; en el otro, hay un muchacho. Ezequiel se acerca a él.

Ezequiel looks at the piece of paper, it has a large number 12 printed on it. He leaves the office and goes to the elevator. He goes up to the seventh floor. There, he looks for office 78. Inside the office, there are many people sitting, waiting. There are two desks. One is empty; in the other, there is a young man. Ezequiel approaches him.

—Mucho gusto —le dice.

"Nice to meet you," he says.

—¡Hola! —dice el muchacho—. ¿Su número?

"Hello!" says the young man. "Your number?"

Ezequiel le muestra el número 12.

Ezekiel shows him the number 12.

El muchacho, entonces, señala una pantalla en la pared, que muestra un el 3.

The man points to a screen on the wall, which shows a 3.

—Tiene que esperar, señor —le dice a Ezequiel.

"You have to wait, sir," he says to Ezequiel.

—Pero yo… —dice él.

"But I…" he says.

—Tiene que esperar a su turno, ¡sin excepciones! —dice el muchacho.

"You have to wait for your turn, no exceptions!" says the young man.

—¡Bueno! Esperaré —dice Ezequiel. Está muy enfadado.

"Okay! I'll wait," says Ezequiel. He is very annoyed.

Los números avanzan lentamente. Después de media hora, la pantalla muestra el número 12. Ezequiel se pone de pie y va hasta el muchacho.

The numbers move forward slowly. After half an hour, the screen shows the number 12. Ezequiel stands up and goes to the man.

—Ahora sí es su turno —dice el muchacho—. ¿Cómo está?

"Now it's your turn," says the young man. "How are you?"

—No muy bien —dice Ezequiel—. He pasado más de una hora dando vueltas por este edificio para llegar hasta aquí. ¿Usted cómo está?

"Not very well," Ezequiel says. "I've spent over an hour walking around this building to get here. How are you?"

—Bueno, sinceramente, tampoco estoy muy bien. El empleado nuevo que debería estar aquí trabajando conmigo aún no llega.

"Well, honestly, I'm not so well either. The new employee who should be here working with me has not arrived yet."

—Lo sé —dice Ezequiel.

"I know," Ezequiel says.

—¿Lo sabe? ¿Cómo lo sabe? —pregunta el muchacho.

"You know? How do you know?" asks the young man.

—¡Yo soy el empleado nuevo! —dice Ezequiel.

"I am the new employee!" says Ezequiel.

Chapter 7 - Numbers

Asking someone's age, indicating an address, shopping, asking for a price... What do these actions have in common?

For all of them, numbers are essential! In this episode, we will learn the basic Spanish numbers.

One is *uno*. Pretty simple, right? Not quite... In Spanish we also have the indefinite articles *un* (masculine) and *una* (feminine), equivalents to English *a* or *an*. We'll learn more about indefinite articles in chapter 9. For now, all you need to know that *un* and *una* mean both *one* and *a*.

For example:

Una doctora y un enfermero me cuidaron - A doctor and a nurse looked after me

Tengo cinco amigos varones y solo una amiga mujer - I have five male friends and only one female friend.

Also, just as in English, in Spanish *one* can be used as a pronoun. For example:

Uno puede cansarse mucho al subir esa colina - One can get really tired walking up that hill

Let's see the following numbers, up to fifteen:

Two is *dos*.

Three is *tres*.

Four is *cuatro*.

Five is *cinco*.

Six is *seis*.

Seven is *siete*.

Eight is *ocho*.

Nine is *nueve*.

Ten is *diez*.

Eleven is *once*.

Twelve is *doce*.

Thirteen is *trece*.

Fourteen is *catorce*.

And fifteen is *quince*.

It's easy to remember numbers from sixteen to nineteen, because they have the same root: *dieci-* plus the numbers six to nine.

Sixteen is *dieciséis*.

Seventeen is *diecisiete*.

Eighteen is *dieciocho*.

Nineteen is *diecinueve*.

Twenty is *veinte*.

Now, let's see how to use the Spanish numbers in twenty example sentences:

1 a 10 - **1 to 10**

Hay un perro en la esquina y dos en la calle - There is one dog in the corner and two on the street

Tengo dos hermanos - I have two brothers

Ella me llama tres veces al día - She calls me three times every day

Esta receta lleva seis huevos - This recipe uses six eggs

La pizza tiene ocho porciones - The pizza has eight slices

El disco tiene nueve canciones - The album has nine songs

10 a 20 - **10 to 20**

¡Te espero a las once! - I'll be waiting for you at eleven!

El almuerzo es a las doce en punto - Lunch is at twelve o'clock

Vuelvo en quince minutos - I'll be back in fifteen minutes

El árbol mide diecisiete metros - The tree is seventeen meters tall

Él cumple dieciocho - He's turning eighteen

Hay diecinueve alumnos en mi curso - There are nineteen students in my class

20 a 30 - **20 to 30**

A los veintiuno, me mudé a un apartamento - At twenty-one, I moved into an apartment

Esa ciudad está a veintidós kilómetros - That city is twenty-two kilometres away

Un día tiene veinticuatro horas - One day has twenty-four hours

Ellos llevan veinticinco años de casados - They have been married for twenty-five years

Febrero tiene veintiocho días - February has twenty-eight days

El libro tiene veintinueve capítulos - The book has twenty-nine chapters

30 a 100 - **30 to 100**

Él tiene treinta camisas - He has thirty shirts

Hay cuarenta invitados - There are forty guests

Hay cincuenta personas en el avión - There are fifty people on the plane

Tengo sesenta centavos - I have sixty cents

Mi padre tiene setenta años - My father is seventy years old

El ochenta por ciento del grupo son mujeres - Eighty percent of the group are women

Este bolso cuesta noventa dólares - This bag costs ninety dollars

Tengo noventa y nueve centavos - I have ninety-nine cents

100 a 1000 - **100 to 1000**

Hay cien años en un siglo - There are a hundred years in a century

El mundo tiene ciento noventa y tres países - The world has one hundred and ninety-three countries

Un año tiene trescientos sesenta y cinco días - A year has three hundred and sixty-five days

La masa pesa cuatrocientos gramos - The dough weights four hundred grams

Mi cuento tiene novecientas palabras - My short story is nine-hundred-words long

¡Te lo he dicho mil veces! - I've told you this a thousand times!

1000 a 100000 - **1,000 to 100,000**

Miami está a mil setecientos kilómetros de Nueva York - Miami is one thousand seven hundred kilometers from New York

Nací en mil novecientos ochenta - I was born in nineteen eighty

Hay tres mil seiscientos kilómetros - There are three thousand six hundred kilometers

En la colmena hay treinta mil abejas - There are thirty thousand bees in the hive

Tengo cincuenta mil dólares - I have fifty thousand dollars

En el campo hay noventa mil árboles - In the field there are ninety thousand trees

100000 a 1000000 - **100,000 to 1,000,000**

Allí viven cien mil personas - A hundred thousand people live there

Esa casa cuesta doscientos mil dólares - That house costs two hundred thousand dollars

La luz viaja a trescientos mil kilómetros por segundo - Light travels at three hundred thousand kilometers per second

El periódico vendió quinientos mil ejemplares - The newspaper sold five hundred thousand copies

Esa cantante tiene ochocientos mil seguidores - That singer has eight hundred thousand followers

Ese estado tiene un millón de habitantes - That state has a million inhabitants

Vocabulario relacionado - **Related vocabulary**

Voy a contar hasta diez - I'm going to count to ten

Joaquín está aprendiendo a sumar - Joaquin is learning how to add numbers

Mi madre tiene cero paciencia - My mother has zero patience

Tengo una calculadora para multiplicar - I have a calculator to multiply

Sé hacer divisiones complejas - I can do complex divisions

Resta la diferencia - Subtract the difference

Chapter 8 - Months and Days of the Week

While travelling, it's particularly important to know what day it is.

For example, you need to be able to answer questions like *¿Cuándo es tu vuelo?* (When is your flight?) and *¿Hasta cuándo te quedas aquí?* (How long are you staying here?).

Let's start with the days of the week!

Monday is *lunes.*

Tuesday is *martes.*

Wednesday is *miércoles.*

Thursday is *jueves.*

Friday is *viernes.*

Saturday is *sábado.*

Sunday is *domingo.*

'Today' is *hoy*. 'Yesterday' is *ayer*. 'Tomorrow' is *mañana* (it's the same word as 'morning').

To ask when something happened, we say *cuándo*. For example: *¿Cuándo llega tu hermano?* (When is your brother arriving?).

The seasons are *verano* (Summer), *otoño* (Autumn), *invierno* (Winter) and *primavera* (Spring). If you're travelling to another hemisphere, the seasons will be the opposite!

But, luckily, the months of the year are the same around the globe:

January is *enero.*

February is *febrero.*

March is *marzo.*

April is *abril.*

May is *mayo.*

June is *junio.*

July is *julio.*

August is *agosto.*

September is *septiembre.*

October is *octubre.*

November is *noviembre.*

December is *diciembre.*

Except for January (*enero*), they're pretty similar, right?

Learn some more useful vocabulary to talk about days, weeks, months and seasons with the following sentences:

Días de la semana - **Days of the week**

El lunes comienzan las clases - Classes start on Monday

Hoy es martes - Today is Tuesday

Los miércoles son mis días libres - Wednesdays are my days off

¡Me encantan los jueves! - I love Thursdays!

Los viernes me divierto - On Fridays I have fun

Los sábados salgo - On Saturdays I go out

Los domingos miro películas - On Sundays I watch movies

Meses - **Months**

Enero es el primer mes del año - January is the first month of the year

Febrero es un mes corto - February is a short month

Este año, febrero tiene veintinueve días - This year, February has twenty-nine days

Mi madre nació en marzo - My mother was born in March

Mis vacaciones son en abril - My holidays are in April

Mi hermana se casa en mayo - My sister is getting married in May

En junio hace calor en el hemisferio norte - June is hot in the northern hemisphere

Julio es mi mes favorito - July is my favorite month

En el hemisferio sur, julio es frío - In the southern hemisphere, July is a cold month

Viajaré en agosto - I am going to travel in August

Trabajo aquí desde septiembre - I've been working here since September

En septiembre entraré a la universidad - In September I will go to university

En octubre es la Noche de Brujas - Halloween is in October

En noviembre, suelo estar muy ocupado - In November, I am usually very busy

En diciembre festejamos Navidad - In December we celebrate Christmas

Diciembre es el último mes del año - December is the last month of the year

Estaciones - Seasons

En invierno cae nieve - Snow falls in the Winter

El invierno es duro - Winter is harsh

Me encanta el otoño - I love the Fall

La primavera es mi estación favorita - Spring is my favorite season

En primavera, hay flores - In Spring, there are flowers

El verano es caluroso - Summer is hot

Adverbios de tiempo - Time adverbs

Hoy es un día especial - Today is a special day

Ayer fui al parque - Yesterday I went to the park

Mañana iré a pescar - Tomorrow i will go fishing

El mes pasado viajé a Londres - Last month I traveled to London

El año que viene visitaré Bruselas - Next year I will visit Brussels

Todavía tengo mucho trabajo - I still have a lot of work

¡Ven ahora! - Come now!

Ya quiero irme - I want to go right now

Anoche apenas dormí - I barely slept last night

Día por medio, voy al gimnasio - Every other day, I go to the gym

Siempre canto mientras cocino - I always sing while I cook

La segunda quincena de junio es calurosa - The second half of June is hot

De vez en cuando, bailo - Every so often, I dance

Por lo general, como verduras - I usually eat vegetables

Nunca me acuesto tarde - I never go to bed late

Siempre me levanto muy temprano - I always get up very early

Habitualmente limpio mi casa - I usually clean my house

Enseguida lo atiendo, señor - I'll take care of you right away, sir

Aún no tengo la nota del examen - I still don't have the exam grade

Una vez por semana, pido comida a domicilio - Once a week I order takeaway food

Tres veces por semana, voy a natación - Three times a week I go swimming

Chapter 9 - Indefinite Articles

We mentioned the indefinite articles in chapter 7, the one about numbers. That is because number one (*uno*) is very similar to the masculine indefinite articles *un* and *una*, which also mean *one*.

Now we'll deal with the articles in more detail.

In English, we have the indefinite article 'a', which becomes 'an' before vowels. For plural nouns, we use adjectives 'some' and 'any', as in *I have an apple* and *I have some apples*.

In Spanish, we have four indefinite articles: *un*, *una*, *unos* and *unas*.

For masculine singular nouns, we use *un*, as in *Me compré un auto* (I bought a car).

Before feminine singular nouns, we use *una*, as in *Me senté en una silla* (I sat on a chair).

To talk about masculine plural nouns, we need *unos*, as in *Encontré unos botones* (I found some buttons).

Finally, for feminine plural nouns, we use *unas*, as in *Me lastimé con unas ramas* (I got hurt with some branches).

As it happens with the definite article for feminine singular nouns *la*, *una* becomes *un* before feminine nouns that start with a stressed A or HA. That is why we say *un hacha* (an axe), even though it's a feminine noun.

Now, practice listening to the indefinite articles with this short story:

El viaje a la playa - **The trip to the beach**

Susana, la mamá de Martín, prepara todo para el viaje a la playa.

Susana, Martín's mother, prepares everything for the trip to the beach.

Ya tiene los sanguches adentro del tupper, ya cargó el tanque de gasolina del coche y ya puso la sombrilla y las reposeras en el maletero. Solo falta preparar el equipaje.

She already has the sandwiches ready inside the tupper, she has already filled the car's gas tank and she has already put the umbrella and the chairs inside the trunk. She only has to get the luggage ready.

—Martín, recuerda: pon en tu maleta solamente lo importante —dice Susana.

"Martin, remember: pack only what is important," says Susana.

Martín asiente y entra en su habitación. Tiene una gran maleta roja abierta sobre la cama, y una pila de ropa y juguetes lista para seleccionar. Es la primera vez que hace la maleta solo.

Martín nods and goes into his room. He has a large red suitcase open on the bed, and a pile of clothes and toys ready to pick from. It is his first time packing alone.

—Solo lo importante —repite Martín mientras mira sus cosas.

"Only what's important," Martin repeats as he looks through his things.

Pone primero la ropa: un traje de baño azul, un traje de baño negro, unas cuantas camisetas, un abrigo, un pantalón, unas sandalias, un par de zapatillas con rueditas y una campera de lluvia. Y ropa interior, por supuesto.

First, packs his clothes: a blue bathing suit, a black bathing suit, a few T-shirts, a coat, pants, sandals, a pair of shoes with wheels, and a rain jacket. And underwear, of course.

La maleta está llena hasta la mitad. Eso significa que todavía puede poner más cosas.

The suitcase is half full. That means that he can still put more things inside.

—También tengo que llevar algo para divertirme durante los días de lluvia —se dice Martín.

"I also have to take something to have fun on rainy days," Martín says to himself.

Entonces pone en la maleta un mazo de cartas, un libro de misterios, una colección de sus historietas favoritas, unos cuantos juegos de mesa y una libreta para dibujar.

Then, he packs a deck of cards, a mystery book, a collection of his favorite comic books, some board games, and a sketchbook.

Ahora la maleta está casi llena. Los juegos de mesa y los libros ocupan mucho lugar.

Now the suitcase is almost full. The board games and the books take up a lot of space.

—¡Casi me olvido de la pelota! —dice de repente Martín.

"I almost forgot about the ball!" Martin says suddenly.

Entonces toma una pelota de fútbol y trata de meterla en la maleta. Pero no entra: hay demasiada ropa. Martín saca entonces una camiseta, un juego de ropa interior y la campera de lluvia. Pero no alcanza.

So he takes a soccer ball and tries to put it in the suitcase. But it doesn't fit: there are too many clothes. Martín then takes out a T-shirt, a set of underwear and the rain jacket. But it is not enough.

Entonces Martín da vuelta la maleta y vuelve a empezar.

Martín then turns the suitcase over and starts again.

—Una pelota, una camiseta, un libro, un mazo de cartas —dice Martín mientras guarda las cosas—. Y por supuesto, un disfraz. No quiero estar desprevenido.

"A ball, a T-shirt, a book, a deck of cards," Martín says as he packs everything inside. "And, of course, a costume. I don't want to be caught off-guard."

A Martín le encantan las fiestas de disfraces. También le gustan las películas de vaqueros, y por eso guarda un sombrero de ala ancha y un arma de juguete. Y a su muñeco favorito, claro, el vaquero.

Martin loves costume parties. He also likes cowboy movies, which is why he also packs a cowboy hat and a toy gun. And his favorite doll, of course, the cowboy.

—Martín, ¿has terminado? —pregunta Susana, entrando en la habitación.

"Martin, are you done?" Susana asks, entering the room.

—¡Sí! ¡Ya está todo listo! —exclama el muchacho, orgulloso.

"Yes! All done!" the boy exclaims, with pride.

—¿Puedo ver tu maleta? —pregunta Susana.

"May I see your suitcase?" Susana asks.

La madre abre la maleta y ve lo que hay dentro: ¡son solo juguetes!

The mother opens the suitcase and takes a look inside: there are only toys!

—Martín, ¡te he dicho que pongas lo importante! —dice Susana—. Ropa, un cepillo de dientes y unos pocos juguetes. A ver, te ayudo.

"Martin, I told you to pack only what's important!" Susana says. Her clothes, a toothbrush and a few toys. Let's see, I'll help you.

Poco después ambos suben al coche, listos para salir. Martín ya tiene puesto el cinturón de seguridad.

Soon after, they both get in the car, ready to go. Martín is already fastening his seat belt.

—¿Todo listo? —pregunta Martín—. ¿Tenemos todo lo importante?

"All ready?" Martin asks. "Do we have what's important?"

Su madre mira a su alrededor y exclama:

—¡Nos faltó lo más importante de todo! ¡Las maletas siguen en la casa!

His mother looks around and says: "We're missing the most important thing of all! The suitcases are still in the house!"

Chapter 10 - Basic Nouns

All nouns in Spanish have a gender, that is, they are either masculine or feminine.

Yes, even the ones referring to food and parts of the body. It is very important to know the gender of the nouns you are using, because they have to match the articles and the adjectives around them.

Nouns are also affected by number (they can be singular or plural), just like in English.

One simple rule to determine the gender of a noun is paying attention to its ending. Nouns ending in A tend to be feminine, like *casa* (house), and nouns ending in O tend to be masculine, like *cuarto* (room).

However, there are exceptions to this rule: there are feminine nouns that end with an *o* and masculine nouns that end with an *a*; and there are lots of nouns that don't end with either.

The only way to learn the genders of nouns is with practica and vocabulary acquisition, which you can get from books, movies, articles, songs and, of course, talking with Spanish-speaking people!

Of course, when in doubt, you can always check the noun online.

Now, let's learn some basic nouns and their genders with 50 example sentences:

Sustantivos en la comida - **Food nouns**

La comida es deliciosa - Food is delicious

El desayuno debe incluir frutas - Breakfast must include fruits

El almuerzo es a la una - Lunch is at one

Ella bebe el café en la merienda - She drinks her coffee at tea time

En España, la cena es más tarde - In Spain, dinner is later

No me gusta la sopa - I don't like soup

Me encantan las salchichas - I love sausages

A mi hermano pequeño no le gusta el tomate - My little brother doesn't like tomato

Los cereales son muy ricos - Cereals are delicious

El jugo de manzana es mi favorito - Apple juice is my favorite

Sustantivos de la casa - **Home nouns**

Esta es la habitación más grande de la casa - This is the largest room in the house

Hay una mesa enorme en la cocina - There is a huge table in the kitchen

Disculpe, ¿dónde está el baño? - Excuse me, where is the restroom?

La sala de tu casa es muy moderna - The living room of your house is very modern

La lámpara está en la mesa de noche - The lamp is on the bedside table

Esa silla no es muy cómoda - That chair is not very comfortable

Hoy vi unas alfombras hermosas en la tienda - Today I saw some beautiful rugs in the store

Esa es una puerta de vidrio - That's a glass door

Las ventanas son oscuras - The windows are dark

Me gustan los pisos de madera - I like wooden floors

Sustantivos del cuerpo - **Body nouns**

El bebé tiene las manos pequeñas - The baby has small hands

Tengo la mejillas coloradas - I have red cheeks

Dumbo tenía las orejas grandes - Dumbo had big ears

Los humanos tenemos las piernas largas - Humans have long legs

Mi tobillo está adolorido - My ankle is sore

¡Me duele la cabeza! - I have a headache!

El perro tiene la nariz fría - The dog's nose is cold

Mis ojos son marrones - My eyes are brown

La boca del niño es enorme - The kid's mouth is huge

El hada de los dientes vendrá esta noche - The tooth fairy will come tonight

Sustantivos animales - **Animals nouns**

Esos perros son muy tiernos - Those dogs are very cute

Esas gatas están cazando ratones - Those cats are hunting mice

La paloma descansa en su nido - The dove is resting in its nest

En los Andes hay muchos cóndores - In the Andes there are many condors

El loro verde habla sin cesar - The green parrot talks incessantly

Las serpientes se arrastran - Snakes crawl

La vaca vive en el campo - The cow lives in the field

Las ovejas tienen mucha lana - Sheep have a lot of wool

Me monto en el caballo - I ride the horse

El caballito de mar vive en el océano - The hippocampus lives in the ocean

Sustantivos de la calle - **Street nouns**

La tienda está en la esquina - The store is at the corner

¡No corras en la calle! - Don't run on the street!

El semáforo está en verde - The traffic light is green

Camino por la acera - I walk on the sidewalk

El coche va por la autopista - The car is on the highway

Mi hermana espera el tren en el andén - My sister is waiting for the train on the platform

El autobús me lleva a la escuela - The bus takes me to school

El metro es muy rápido - The metro is very fast

Esos carteles indican la velocidad máxima - Those signs show the maximum speed

Mi mamá va al volante - My mom is at the wheel

Chapter 11 - Basic Adjectives

Adjectives are the words we use to describe nouns and pronouns, like *alto* (tall), *feo* (ugly) or *amarillo* (yellow).

In Spanish, adjectives normally are placed *after* nouns. For example: *Tengo una pelota verde* is *I have a green ball*. *Verde* means *green* and *pelota* means *ball*. *Pelota verde* is *green ball*.

Adjectives in Spanish have to agree in gender and number with the noun or pronoun they are describing. Adjectives ending in *o* are masculine and adjectives ending in *a* are feminine. For example: *Él es un hombre malo* is *He is a bad man*; and *Ella es una mujer mala* is *She is a bad woman*. *Malo* and *mala* are the masculine and feminine translations of *bad*.

There are also some adjectives that are invariable: they don't change depending on the gender of the noun, like *enorme* (huge), *feliz* (happy) and *fácil* (easy).

Finally, to make an adjective plural, you just need to add *s* or the letters *es* at the end *enorme* becomes *enormes*, *fácil* becomes *fáciles* and *mala* becomes *malas*.

See other adjectives in the following example sentences:

Adjetivos y ropa - Adjectives and clothing

La blusa es muy pequeña - The blouse is too small

Mis pantalones vaqueros son muy viejos - My jeans are very old

Tus plantas son hermosas - Your plants are beautiful

Tengo tres chaquetas amarillas - I have three yellow jackets

Este pantalón es feo - These trousers are ugly

Ese suéter es muy suave - That sweater is very soft

Esta sudadera es muy liviana - This T-shirt is very light

Mi cinturón está roto - My belt is broken

Mi sombrero está gastado - My hat is worn out

Este traje es demasiado abrigado - This suit is too warm

Adjetivos y lugares - Adjectives and places

Yo soy de un pueblo muy pequeño - I am from a very small town

Nueva York es una ciudad enorme - New York is a huge city

Ese país es bello - That country is beautiful

Ese prado es muy verde - That meadow is very green

Las cascadas son muy poderosas - The waterfalls are very powerful

Las montañas son increíbles - The mountains are awesome

El desierto es peligroso por la noche - The desert is dangerous at night

París es elegante - Paris is elegant

Pekín es una ciudad muy moderna - Beijing is a very modern city

En Buenos Aires hay grandes avenidas - In Buenos Aires there are big avenues

Adjetivos y personas - Adjectives and people

Los amigos de mi hermana son muy simpáticos - My sister's friends are very nice

Mis hermanos son pelirrojos - My brothers are redheads

Mi amiga Teresa es muy graciosa - My friend Teresa is very funny

Mi primo es un hombre muy serio - My cousin is a very serious man

Los vecinos de enfrente son amables - Neighbors across the street are kind

La profesora de Ciencias es muy comprensiva - The science teacher is very understanding

Mi abuelo era muy estudioso - My grandfather studied very hard

Mi amigo Isidro es un cantante talentoso - My friend Isidro is a talented singer

Mi tía es una doctora prestigiosa - My aunt is a prestigious doctor

Kevin es un mal bailarín - Kevin is a bad dancer

Adjetivos y comida - Adjectives and food

Estos tacos están muy picantes - These tacos are very spicy

El pastel está congelado - The cake is frozen

La salsa está agria - The sauce is sour

Este postre está muy dulce - This dessert is very sweet

El café es muy caro en esta tienda - Coffee is very expensive in this shop

Las hamburguesas son redondas - Burgers are round

La pizza está aceitosa - The pizza is oily

Me gusta el té helado - I like iced tea

El helado más sabroso es el de vainilla - The most tasty ice cream flavor is vanilla

El tomate es rojo - The tomato is red

Adjetivos y animales - Adjectives and animals

Ese gato es blanco - That cat is white

La mirada del caballo es profunda - The horse's gaze is deep

Los animales son salvajes - Animals are wild

La tortuga es muy lenta - The turtle is very slow

El perro es miedoso - The dog is fearful

Ese cocodrilo está enojado - That crocodile is angry

El zorro enseña sus dientes afilados - The fox shows its sharp teeth

Los canguros australianos son muy veloces - Australian kangaroos are very fast

La cola del ratón es larga - The mouse's tail is long

El león es muy viejo - The lion is very old

Chapter 12 - Basic Verbs

While in English verb conjugations are straightforward and simple, Spanish conjugations are quite complex. But don't worry, in this lesson we'll start approaching them.

Verbs in Spanish change depending on the person: *who* or *what* is doing the action. And, since usually in Spanish that person is not explicit, the conjugation of the verb will let you know who is doing the action. For example, we can say *En la mañana, bebo leche* (In the morning, I drink milk). The word *yo* (I) is not in the sentence, but we know who the subject is (I) because of the conjugation of the verb *beber* (to drink).

Verbs also change depending on the tense, that is to say, depending on *when* the action is taking place. There are three basic tenses: present, past and future. English also conjugates verbs based on person and tense, yes!; however, Spanish has a lot more variations. But let's start with the very basics.

Let's start with the *infinitive form*.

The infinitive form of a verb is the one that doesn't refer to any person or any time, equivalent to saying 'to walk' in English. In Spanish, all verbs in the infinitive form are formed by a root plus one of the following endings: AR, like *amar* (to love); ER, like *comer* (to eat); and IR, like *vivir* (to live).

In regular verbs, the root stays always the same, and the ending changes when we conjugate the verb, following a pattern that depends on whether the infinitive finishes in AR, ER or IR. There are also irregular verbs, but we'll deal with them in due time.

These are some of the most common Spanish verbs:

Ser means to be, for permanent traits.

Estar means to be, for temporary conditions.

Tener means to have.

Hacer means to do.

Saber means to know.

Decir means to say.

Venir means to come.

Ir means to go.

Hablar means to speak.

Dar means to give.

Tomar means to take.

Find these and more basic Spanish verbs in this short story:

El vendedor de aspiradoras - **The vacuum cleaner salesman**

Alberto toca el timbre de la casa. Una voz áspera suena desde el otro lado de la puerta.

Alberto rings the house bell. A harsh voice sounds from the other side of the door.

—¿Quién es? —dice la voz. Parece que la voz pertenece a una mujer anciana.

"Who is it?" says the voice. It seems that the voice belongs to an old woman.

—Buenos días —dice Alberto—. Soy Alberto Domínguez, y vengo a hacerle una oferta única.

"Good morning," says Alberto. I am Alberto Domínguez, and I have come to make you a unique offer.

La puerta se abre un poco.

The door opens up a little bit.

—¿Qué cosa? —pregunta la mujer.

"What is it?" the woman asks.

—Señora, escuche bien —continúa Alberto—. Tengo aquí una Zonda 9000, la mejor aspiradora del mercado. Tome, vea qué liviana es.

"Ma'am, listen well," Alberto continues. I have here a Zonda 9000, the best vacuum cleaner on the market. Take it, see how light it is.

Esa es una vieja táctica: cuando el cliente toma la aspiradora, está obligado a dejarlo pasar. Y funciona esta vez. La mujer abre la puerta, hace entrar a Alberto, y la vuelve a cerrar. ¡Con llave!

That's an old tactic: when the customer picks up the vacuum, they are forced to let him into the house. And it works this time. The woman opens the door, lets Alberto in, and closes it again. With a key!

"Una mujer precavida", piensa Alberto.

"A cautious woman," Alberto thinks.

El pasillo de entrada es amplio, lleno de cuadros y estatuillas. Hay un fuerte olor a basura, quizás incluso a... algo podrido.

The entrance hall is wide, full of paintings and statuettes. There is a strong smell of garbage, maybe even... something rotten.

—Es muy liviana —dice la señora, levantando la aspiradora—. ¿Quiere pasar al salón?

"It's very light," says the lady, picking up the vacuum cleaner. "Do you want to come into the living room?"

—Encantado —responde Alberto.

"Delighted," Alberto replies.

La decoración del salón es extraña: dos cabezas de ciervo y una cabeza de oso cuelgan de la pared del fondo. Sobre la pared lateral, ¡hay seis rifles!

The decoration of the living room is strange: two deer heads and a bear head hang on the back wall. On the side wall, there are six rifles!

—¿Su marido caza? —pregunta Alberto.

"Does your husband hunt?" Alberto asks.

—No, querido —responde la mujer—. Mi esposo ya está muerto... y estos son todos míos. Me gustan las presas *grandes*. —Una amplia sonrisa sin dientes aparece en su rostro.

"No, dear," the woman replies. "My husband is dead... and these are all mine. I like big *prey." A wide toothless smile appears on her face.*

—Lo siento... —dice Alberto con incomodidad—. Bueno, en cuanto a la aspiradora... Yo le puedo dar un treinta por ciento de descuento en efectivo, ¿sabe?

"I'm sorry" Alberto says, uneasily "Well, as for the vacuum cleaner... I can give you a thirty percent cash discount, you know?"

—Muy interesante —dice la señora, alzando la aspiradora una vez más. Alberto nota que la mujer, aunque es anciana, es ágil y rápida—. ¿La aspiradora tiene problemas con las cenizas?

"Very interesting," says the lady, lifting the vacuum cleaner once more. Alberto notices that the woman, although she is old, is agile and fast. "Could the vacuum cleaner have a problem picking up ash?"

—¡¿Cómo?! —pregunta Alberto, desconcertado.

"What?!" Alberto asks, puzzled.

—Cenizas —responde la señora—. A veces quemo partes de los cuerpos... De los animales que cazo, claro. Tengo un incinerador en el fondo.

"Ashes," the lady replies. "I sometimes burn body parts... Of the animals I hunt, of course. I have an incinerator in the back."

"Otra vez esa sonrisa", piensa Alberto. "No me hace gracia".

"That smile again," thinks Alberto. "It is not funny."

—No tiene problemas con las cenizas —continúa Alberto mientras empieza a sudar—. Además, la Zonda 9000...

"It has no problem with the ashes," Alberto continues, as he begins to sweat. "Also, the Zonda 9000..."

—Disculpe, ¿quiere un té? —interrumpe la señora—. Soy muy buena preparando té. La gente siempre dice que viene con algo *extra*.

"Excuse me, do you want some tea?" the lady interrupts him. "I am very good at making tea. People always say it comes with something... extra."

—Sí. Gracias —responde Alberto automáticamente.

"Yes. Thank you," Alberto answers automatically.

La anciana se levanta con sorprendente agilidad y va hacia la cocina. Todavía tiene la aspiradora en la mano. Sin embargo, Alberto no está preocupado por la aspiradora. Él piensa en la taza de té y el ingrediente "extra", en la mirada de la anciana y en su extraña sonrisa. Piensa en las "presas grandes" y en los rifles. Piensa en el incinerador del fondo.

The old woman gets up with surprising agility and goes to the kitchen. She still has the vacuum cleaner in her hand. However, Alberto is not worried about the vacuum cleaner. He thinks of the cup of tea and the "extra" ingredient, of the old woman's gaze and her strange smile. He thinks of the "big prey" and the rifles. He thinks of the incinerator in the back.

Alberto está empapado de sudor; tiene calor y necesita aire. Se acerca, entonces, a la ventana de la sala, que está abierta.

Alberto is drenched in sweat; he is hot and needs air. He then goes over to the living room window, which is open.

Sin pensarlo demasiado, sale por la ventana y se aleja corriendo por la calle.

Without thinking too much about it, he climbs out the window and runs off down the street.

La señora vuelve y mira su sala vacía.

—Siempre funciona —dice, mientras sostiene su aspiradora nueva.

The lady returns and looks at her empty living room.

"It always works," she says, as she holds her new vacuum cleaner.

Chapter 13 - The Present Tense (part I)

As we said in the previous lesson, in Spanish, we conjugate verbs in present, past or future tenses. And, ss there is no better time than now, we'll start with the present!

We use the present simple tense to talk about what happens on a regular basis; for example: *Los sábados visito a mi abuela* (On Saturdays I visit my grandmother). Also, we use it to talk about what is true at the moment and what is generally true; for example: *Me gusta la música* (I like music).

Both *cantar* and *gustar* end in AR, so they belong to the first conjugation. All regular verbs ending in AR will change in the same way at the time of conjugating. Let's see how.

If we drop the AR ending, we are left with the root of the verb: *cant-*.

For the present simple of the first person *yo*, we add *-o*: *yo canto*.

For the present simple of the first person *nosotras* and *nosotros*, we add *-amos*: *nosotros cantamos*.

For the present simple of the second person *tú*, we add *-as*: *tú cantas*.

For the present simple of the second person *vos*, we add *-ás*: *vos cantás*.

For the present simple of the third person *usted*, we add *-a*: *usted canta*.

For the present simple of the second person *vosotras* and *vosotros*, we add *-áis*: *vosotros cantáis*.

For the present simple of the third person *ella* and *él*, we add *-a*: *él canta*.

For the present simple of the third person *ellas* and *ellos*, we add *-an*: *ellos cantan*.

Learn more basic regular and irregular Spanish verbs in the present tense in the following 50 example sentences:

Verbos regulares terminados en AR en presente - Regular verbs ending in AR in the present tense

Yo preparo un pastel de chocolate delicioso - I prepare a delicious chocolate cake

Siempre abrazo a mi gato siamés - I always hug my Siamese cat

Los sábados, cuido a mi sobrino - On Saturdays, I take care of my nephew

Tú miras películas de vaqueros en la tele - You watch cowboy movies on TV

Tú estudias para tu examen de Historia - You study for your History exam

Tú mezclas los ingredientes - You mix the ingredients

Vos alimentás a tu gata - You feed your cat

Vos te maquillás - You wear makeup

¿Usted lleva el postre? - Do you bring the dessert?

Él espera el autobús para ir a trabajar - He waits for the bus to go to work

Walter camina despacio - Walter walks slowly

Lara baila flamenco - Lara dances flamenco

Mi perro se nada en el mar - My dog swims in the sea

La doctora cura al herido - The doctor heals the wounded

El doctor opera un paciente - The doctor operates on a patient

El autobús avanza - The bus moves forward

Mi hermana pequeña dibuja un árbol - My little sister draws a tree

Mi hermano ama los videojuegos - Mi brother loves video games

Nosotros cantamos una canción - We sing a song

Mis amigos siempre luchan por sus sueños - My friends always fight for their dreams

Los domingos almorzamos en familia - On Sundays we have lunch as a family

Vosotros viajáis a la playa en verano - You travel to the beach in summer

Ellos escuchan su programa de radio favorito - They listen to their favorite radio show

Los perros ladran por la noche - Dogs bark at night

Las flores se marchitan en invierno - Flowers wither in the winter

Verbos irregulares terminados en AR en presente - Irregular verbs ending in AR in the present tense

Yo pruebo la salsa - I taste the sauce

Pienso que eres una buena persona - I think you are a good person

Yo almuerzo muy temprano - I have lunch very early

¡Te lo ruego! - I beg you!

Caliento agua para mi té - I heat water for my tea

Recuerdo mis años de juventud - I remember my years of youth

¡Apuesto que sí! - I bet so!

¿Tú sueñas por las noches? - ¿Do you dream at night?

Tú siempre juegas a las cartas - You always play cards

Tú comienzas la universidad el año que viene - You start college next year

¿Él niega haber estado allí? - Does he deny having been there?

Usted encuentra sus gafas - You find your glasses

Mi perro se revuelca en la alfombra - My dog rolls on the carpet

El niño tiembla cuando hace frío - The kid trembles when it's cold

Él se despierta muy temprano - He wakes up very early

Ella cierra la ventana - She closes the window

Miguel me muestra su nuevo coche - Miguel shows me his new car

Lucía se sienta en el sofá rojo - Lucía sits on the red couch

Rebeca aprueba su examen de Arte - Rebeca passes her Art exam

Los globos revientan - The balloons pop

Esos pájaros vuelan muy alto - Those birds fly so high

El presidente gobierna el país - The president rules the country

La vaca da leche - The cow gives milk

Tus amigos piensan darte una sorpresa - Your friends plan to surprise you

Ellos comprueban los hechos - They check the facts

Chapter 14 - Introducing Yourself

Hi! Hello! How are you? Have we met? I think we have, but it's time to learn how to do it again, this time in Spanish!

If you want to introduce yourself, say your name, you can try with these formulas:

Me llamo is I am called.

Mi nombre es is My name is.

Mi apellido es is My surname is.

Me dicen is I go by.

If you want to ask for someone's name, you can try these:

¿Y tú? is 'And you?

¿Cómo te llamas? is What is are you called?

¿Cuál es tu nombre? is What's your name?

¿Cómo te dicen? is 'What's your nickname?'

If you are addressing someone in a formal context, you will want to use: *¿Cómo se llama?* or *¿Cuál es su nombre?* (both meaning 'What's your name?').

If you want to talk about what you do or your profession, you can say:

Soy... (I am...)

Estudio... (I study...)

Quiero ser... (I want to be...)

Trabajo de... (I work as...)

Me dedico a... (I'm in...)

Trabajo en... (I work in...)

If you want to talk about your origins, you can say:

Soy de... (I'm from)

Nací en... (I was born in...)

Soy... (I'm...)

Vivo en... (I live in...)

Hablo... (I speak...)

If you want to talk a bit more about yourself, you can say:

Nací en... (I was born in...)

Me gusta... (I like...)

I am... (I am...)

Tengo 2 hijos. (I have 2 kids)

Tengo 30 años. (I am 30 years old). (If you need to, go back to chapter 7, where we went over the numbers!)

Now, let's practice introductions with these 50 example sentences:

Presentaciones - Presentations

Soy Alfredo, ¿y tú? - I'm Alfredo, and you?

Mi nombre es Paloma, ¿el tuyo? - My name is Paloma, what's yours?

Mi apellido es García - My last name is García

¡Mucho gusto! - Pleased to meet you!

Es un placer conoceros - It is a pleasure to meet you

Mi familia es muy grande - My family is very large

Mi familia está compuesta por mi padre, mi madre, mis dos hermanos y yo - In my family there's my father, my mother, my two brothers and me

¿Cómo se compone tu familia? - How is your family composed?

¿Cómo se llaman tus padres? - What are your parents' names?

¿Cuál es el nombre de tu perro? - What is your dog's name?

Me llamo Roberto, pero todos me dicen Bob - My name is Roberto, but everyone calls me Bob

¿Tienes algún apodo? - Do you have a nickname?

¿Qué nombre le pusiste a tu gato? - What name did you give your cat?

Me dicen Kika, ¿y a ti? - I go by Kika, and you?

Tengo diecinueve años - I'm nineteen years old

¿Qué edad tienes? - How old are you?

¿Cuántos años tiene? - How old are you?

Soy el mayor de mis hermanos - I am the eldest of my brothers

Tengo una hija - I have a daughter

¿Eres mayor de veintiún años? - Are you over twenty-one years old?

Lugares - **Places**

¿De dónde eres? - Where are you from?

Soy de Ciudad de México - I am from Mexico City

¿Vosotros sois de aquí? - Are you from here?

Yo soy de Italia - I am from Italy

Soy alemán - I am German

¿Dónde queda tu ciudad? - Where is your city?

Mi casa está en esa dirección - My house is that way

¿Dónde vives? - Where do you live?

¿Dónde naciste? - Where were you born?

Mi abuela nació en Sudáfrica - My grandmother was born in South Africa

Yo nací en este pueblo - I was born in this town

¿Dónde han nacido tus padres? - Where were your parents born?

Mis abuelos emigraron desde Taiwán - My grandparents emigrated from Taiwan

¿Vos vivís acá? - Do you live here?

Mi casa queda muy cerca - My house is very near

Trabajo y estudios - **Work and studies**

Soy ingeniero, ¿y tú? - I'm an engineer, and you?

Yo trabajo en ese edificio - I work in that building

¿De qué trabajas? - What do you do for work?

¿Qué hacés de tu vida? - What do you do?

¿Tienes empleo? - You have a job?

¿Vos a qué te dedicás? - What do you do for work?

En nuestra familia, nos dedicamos a la industria farmacéutica - In our family, we work in the pharmaceutical industry

Trabajo en una tienda de mascotas - I work in a pet store

¿Dónde trabaja usted? - Where do you work?

Quiero ser cirujana - I want to be a surgeon

Me gustaría estudiar algo divertido - I would like to study something fun

Mi amiga Nora es cocinera - My friend Nora is a cook

Soy reportero y trabajo en un canal de televisión - I am a reporter and I work for a television channel

Hice la carrera de Arquitectura - I completed a degree in Architecture

Estoy estudiando Psicología - I'm studying Psychology

Chapter 15 - The Present Tense (part II)

In the first chapter dedicated to the present tense, we learned how to conjugate verbs whose infinitive ends in -*ar*. Now, we'll learn how to conjugate verbs whose infinitive form ends in -*er*.

And since everyone loves food, we'll use *comer* (to eat) as our model verb.

If we drop the ER ending, we are left with the root of the verb: *com-*.

For the present simple of the first person *yo*, we add -*o*: *yo como*.

For the present simple of the first person *nosotras* and *nosotros*, we add -*emos*: *nosotros comemos*.

For the present simple of the second person *tú*, we add -*es*: *tú comes*.

For the present simple of the second person *vos*, we add -*és*: *vos comés*.

For the present simple of the third person *usted*, we add -*e*: *usted come*.

For the present simple of the second person *vosotras* and *vosotros*, we add -*éis*: *vosotros coméis*.

For the present simple of the third person *ella* and *él*, we add -*e*: *él come*.

For the present simple of the third person *ellas* and *ellos*, we add -*en*: *ellos comen*.

Learn more basic regular and irregular Spanish verbs in the present tense in the following short story:

Boca de fuego - Fire mouth

—Bienvenidos, damas y caballeros, a una nueva edición del concurso Boca de Fuego, el certamen más *picante* de la región —dice Fernando, el relator.

"Welcome, ladies and gentlemen, to a new edition of the Fire Mouth contest, the hottest contest in the region," says Fernando, the host.

—Hoy tenemos participantes de toda la región: Juancho Ramírez, Rulo Pérez, Carlos García, Roberto Paredes y…. Emilio, ¿quién es esa señora? Parece muy mayor.

"Today we have participants from all over the region: Juancho Ramírez, Rulo Pérez, Carlos García, Roberto Paredes and…. Emilio, who is that lady? She looks very old."

—Esa es la señora Molina, mi vecina —dice Emilio, el comentarista—. ¡Tiene noventa y tres años!

"That's Mrs. Molina, my neighbor," says Emilio, the commentator. "She is ninety-three years old!"

—¿Es tu vecina? —pregunta Fernando.

"She's your neighbor?" Fernando asks.

—Sí, y ella puede comer cualquier cosa —responde Emilio—. Y puede beber cualquier cosa también. Puede beberse una barrica de vino entera sin problema.

"Yes, and she can eat anything," Emilio answers. "And she can drink anything too. She can drink a whole barrel of wine without a problem."

—De acuerdo... —dice Fernando, sin creer a su compañero—. Todos estos participantes quieren ganar el título de "Boca de Fuego". Y ya tienen en sus platos algunos de los ajíes más *candentes* del planeta: los *aliento de dragón*. Veo que Juancho muerde uno sin problemas, y mientras tanto Roberto Paredes... ¿Es correcto lo que veo, Emilio?

"Okay..." Fernando says, not believing his partner. "All of these participants want to win the title of 'Fire Mouth.' And they already have some of the hottest peppers on the planet on their plates: the 'Dragon's Breaths.' I see that Juancho bites one without problems, and meanwhile Roberto Paredes... Is what I see correct, Emilio?"

—Así es, Fernando —responde Emilio—. Roberto Paredes palidece. Entiendo que morder un aliento de dragón es básicamente como comer fuego, así que no es ninguna sorpresa. ¡Eso debe *arder*!

"That's right, Fernando," Emilio answers. "Roberto Paredes is turning pale. I understand that biting a 'dragon's breath' is basically like eating fire, so it's no surprise. That must burn!"

—¡Parece que Roberto Paredes abandona la competencia! —dice Fernando—. Y ya estamos en el nivel dos: los camareros ofrecen con pinzas un *ají llamarada*. Solo tocar estos ajíes quema.

"It seems that Roberto Paredes is leaving the competition!" Fernando says. "And we are already at level two: the waiters offer a 'flare chili pepper' using tongs. Just touching these peppers burns."

—Cuando comes uno, se enciende una fogata en tu boca, Fernando —comenta Emilio.

"When you eat one, a fire lights up inside your mouth, Fernando," Emilio comments.

—¡Dios mío! —exclama Fernando—. ¡Carlos García se desvanece! Esto realmente me sorprende. Y, mientras tanto, la señora Molina no parece afectada. Y ya entramos en el nivel 3: los chiles *Krakatoa*.

"Oh, my God!" exclaims Fernando. "Carlos García is vanishing! This really surprises me. And, meanwhile, Mrs. Molina does not seem affected. And we already entered level 3: the Krakatoa peppers.

—La señora Molina sabe lo que hace —responde Emilio—. Créeme, ella ve un Krakatoa y se pone alegre.

"Mrs. Molina knows what she's doing," Emilio answers. "Believe me, she sees a Krakatoa and gets cheerful."

—¡El que no se pone alegre es Rulo Pérez, que abandona el concurso! —interrumpe Fernando—. ¡Esto es un mano a mano entre Juancho Ramírez y la señora Molina! ¡Qué final inesperado!

"The one who is not cheerful is Rulo Pérez, who abandons the contest!" Fernando interrupts him. "This is a heads up between Juancho Ramírez and Mrs. Molina! What an unexpected ending!"

—Inesperado para ti, Fernando —dice Emilio.

"Unexpected for you, Fernando," says Emilio.

—Y ahora viene el plato fuerte de la noche, el verdadero fuego, ¡el chile *Nerón*! —continúa Fernando—. Este ají puede *prender fuego* a *toda* la ciudad. Y Juancho Ramírez lo mete en su boca y… ¡Dios mío! ¡Un médico, por favor!

"And now, the main course of the night, the real fire, the Nerón pepper!" Fernando continues. "This pepper can set the entire city on fire. And Juancho Ramírez puts it in his mouth and… My God! A doctor, please!"

—Eso no es lindo de ver —comenta Emilio.

"That is not pretty to see," says Emilio.

—Es parte del juego —responde Fernando—. La parte mala, claro. Pero esto significa… ¡La señora Molina es la ganadora! Emilio, necesitamos una entrevista con la campeona: nuestra audiencia lo merece.

"It's part of the game," says Fernando. "The bad part, of course. But this means… Mrs. Molina is the winner! Emilio, we need an interview with the champion: our audience deserves it."

—¡Señora Molina! —dice Emilio—. ¡Señora Molina! Soy yo, Emilio.

"Mrs. Molina!" Says Emilio. "Mrs. Molina! It's me, Emilio."

—Hola, querido —dice la señora Molina.

"Hello, dear," says Mrs. Molina.

—Disculpe, pero ¿cómo hace para comer así? —pregunta Emilio—. ¿Le gusta mucho?

"Excuse me, but how do you eat like that?" Emilio asks. "Do you like it a lot?"

—No, en realidad no me gusta tanto —responde la señora Molina—. Pero lo que menos me gusta es perder.

"No, I don't really like it that much," Mrs. Molina replies. "But what I really don't like is losing."

Chapter 16 - Talking about the Family

When talking about yourself and asking about other people's lives, at some point you will need to talk about your family.

The basic family-related vocabulary you will need is this:

familia is family.

madre is mother.

padre is father.

hermana is sister.

hermano is brother.

hija is daughter.

hijo is son.

But families are normally more than that. We have *tías y tíos* (aunts and uncles), *abuelas y abuelos* (grandmothers and grandfathers), *primas y primos* (cousins) and much more!

And, of course, nowadays families are not so schematic. In these 50 example sentences, we'll cover step-parents, half-siblings, in-laws, and even pets!

Familia directa - Close family

Mi padre es cocinero - My father is a cook

Mi madre es doctora - My mother is a doctor

Mi papá canta - My dad sings

Mi mamá lee - My mom reads

Mi hija salta - My daughter jumps

Mi hijo patina - My son skates

Mi esposo es Rubén - My husband is Rubén

A mi marido le gusta ir al cine - My husband likes to go to the movies

Mi esposa es trabajadora - My wife is a hard worker

Mi hermana estudia - My sister studies

Mi hermano juega al vóley - My brother plays volleyball

Mi hermanita ama el chocolate - My little sister loves chocolate

Mi hermanito baila - My little brother dances

Mi medio hermano es cirujano - My half brother is a surgeon

Mi media hermana es periodista - My half sister is a journalist

Mi abuela cocina - My grandmother cooks

Mi abuelo cuenta anécdotas - My grandfather tells anecdotes

Jacinto tiene diez nietos - Jacinto has ten grandchildren

Francisco es mi nieto - Francisco is my grandson

Laura es mi nieta - Laura is my granddaughter

Familia extendida - Extended family

Mi tío es alto - MI uncle is tall

Mi tía es arquitecta - My aunt is an architect

Mi primo juega al básquet - My cousin plays basketball

Mi primito mira televisión - My little cousin watches television

Ayer nació mi sobrino - My nephew was born yesterday

Úrsula es mi sobrina - Úrsula is my niece

¡Mi bisabuelo cumplirá cien años! - My great-grandfather is going to be 100 years old!

Mi bisabuela es amable - My great grandmother is kind

¿Tiene bisnietos, señor? - Do you have great-grandchildren, sir?

Mi tatarabuela era poeta - My great-great-grandmother was a poet

Mi tatarabuelo era muy serio - My great-great-grandfather was very serious

Este año, nacerá su tataranieto - This year, her great-great-grandson will be born

Familia política - In-laws

Mi suegra es simpática - My mother-in-law is nice

Mi suegro adora los perros - My father-in-law loves dogs

A mi cuñado le encanta escribir - My brother-in-law loves writing

Mi cuñada y yo vamos a la playa - My sister-in-law and I go to the beach

Mi padrastro es panadero - My stepfather is a baker

Mi madrastra es profesora - My stepmother is a teacher

Mis hijastros son estudiosos - My stepchildren are studious

Mi hijastra canta - My stepdaughter sings

Mi hermanastra juega al fútbol - My stepsister plays soccer

Mi hermanastro dibuja - My stepbrother draws

Mascotas - Pets

Mi perro se llama Tomi - My dog's name is Tomi

Mi gato es atigrado - My cat is tabby

Mi hámster es peludo - My hamster is furry

Vocabulario relacionado - Related vocabulary

Tomás es mi exesposo - Tomás is my ex-husband

Ella es mi exesposa - She's my ex-wife

Yo soy hijo único - I am an only child

Mi amiga tuvo gemelos - My friend had identical twins

Francisco y Nora son mellizos - Francisco and Nora are twins

Ellos son trillizos - They are triplets

Chapter 17 - The Present Tense (part III)

This is the last chapter dedicated to the Spanish present tense. In this chapter we will learn how to conjugate verbs whose infinitive form ends in -ir.

And since sharing is caring, we'll use *compartir* (to share) as our model verb.

If we drop the IR ending, we are left with the root of the verb: *compart-*.

For the present simple of the first person *yo*, we add -o: *yo comparto*.

For the present simple of the first person *nosotras* and *nosotros*, we add -imos: *nosotros compartimos*.

For the present simple of the second person *tú*, we add -es: *tú compartes*.

For the present simple of the second person *vos*, we add -ís: *vos compartís*.

For the present simple of the third person *usted*, we add -e: *usted comparte*.

For the present simple of the second person *vosotras* and *vosotros*, we add -ís: *vosotros compartís*.

For the present simple of the third person *ella* and *él*, we add -e: *él comparte*.

For the present simple of the third person *ellas* and *ellos*, we add -en: *ellos comparten*.

Learn more basic regular and irregular Spanish verbs in the present tense in the following 50 example sentences:

Verbos regulares terminados en IR en presente - Regular verbs ending in IR in the present tense

Es momento de partir - It is time to go

Ella vive en Noruega - She lives in Norway

Añade una taza de azúcar - Add a cup of sugar

Ellos siempre discuten por todo - They always argue about everything

Van a emitir mi película favorita - They will broadcast my favorite movie

¡Me aburro! - I'm bored!

Abre la puerta - Open the door

El perro se sacude - The dog shakes

Todos aplauden - Everyone is clapping

¡No debes presumir! - You shouldn't brag!

Mi amigo asistió al evento - My friend attended the event

Ese ruido me aturde - That noise is stunning me

Este aparato consume mucha electricidad - This artifact consumes lots of energy

El profesor imparte una clase - The professor teaches a class

¿Vas a escribir un libro? - Are you going to write a book?

Ella exprime las naranjas - She squeezes the oranges

Recibo un paquete - I receive a package

¡Los monstruos no existen! - Monsters don't exist!

Mi cumpleaños coincide con Navidad - My birthday coincides with Christmas

Tengo que imprimir un documento - I have to print a document

Mi hermana sube las escaleras - My sister walks up the stairs

Él cumplió con su palabra - He kept his word

No debes insistir - You shouldn't insist

El barco se hunde - The boat is sinking

Vamos a debatir al respecto - Let's debate about it

Verbos irregulares terminados en IR en presente - Regular verbs ending in IR in the present tense

Voy a la escuela - I go to school

La torre mide cien metros - The tower is 100 metres tall

Me gusta freír las salchichas - I like to fry the sausages

Quiero decir algo - I want to say something

Juana dice siempre la verdad - Juana always says the truth

Me divierto con mis hermanos - I have fun with my brothers

Siempre que te veo, sonrío - Whenever I see you, I smile

Elijo la mejor comida para mi gato - I choose the best food for my cat

¿Cómo luzco? - How do I look?

Ella me pide un favor - She asks me for a favor

Esa aplicación sirve para traducir - This app is used to translate

El río fluye - The river flows

El árbol muere - The tree dies

Me siento muy bien - I feel very good

Deduzco que vosotros sois hermanos - I deduce that you are siblings

Siempre me río contigo - I always laugh with you

¿Oyes ese ruido? - Do you hear that noise?

Ella se viste muy elegante - She dresses very elegant

El perro gruñó - The dog growled

Construyo una casa - I build a house

Él conduce muy despacio - He drives very slowly

La empresa produce ganancias - The company produces profits

Él lo predice - He predicts it

Al salir, cierra la puerta - When you go out, close the door

¡Lo vamos a conseguir! - We will get it!

Chapter 18 - Talking about Work

Whether you're meeting new people, working and travelling or applying to a job in a Spanish-speaking country, you will need to get acquainted with work-related vocabulary.

These are some work-related nouns:

trabajo is *work* or job.

empleo is job.

jefe or *jefa* is boss.

empleado or *empleada* is employee.

colega is colleage.

profesión is profession.

tiempo completo is full time.

jornada parcial is part time.

oficina is office.

puesto or *cargo* is position.

aumento is raise.

promoción is promotion.

currículum or *hoja de vida* is CV.

These are some work-related verbs:

trabajar is to work.

contratar is to hire.

despedir is to fire.

entrevistar is to interview.

recomendar is to recommend

entregar is to deliver.

cumplir is to accomplish.

revisar is to review.

recibir el salario or *recibir el pago* is to get paid.

These are some work-related useful sentences and questions:

¿A qué te dedicas? - What do you do?

¿De qué trabajas? - What do you do for work?

¿Hace cuánto trabajas ahí? - How long have you worked there?

Soy… - I am a…

Yo trabajo en… - I work at…

Mañana tengo que trabajar - Tomorrow I have to work

Learn more work-related vocabulary with this short story:

El turno noche - The night shift

Amalia, Francisco y Jésica están en la sala de descanso de la oficina. Es de noche. Las luces de los coches que pasan por la calle se reflejan en el gran espejo de la sala. Los tres cenan durante un breve recreo.

Amalia, Francisco and Jésica are in the office break room. It is night. The lights of the cars that pass by the street are reflected in the large mirror in the room. The three have dinner during a short break.

—¿Qué piensan del nuevo empleado? —pregunta Amalia.

"What do you guys think of the new employee?" Amalia asks.

—¿Vladimir? —pregunta Jésica.

"Vladimir?" Jésica asks.

—Sí, el nuevo —responde Amalia—. El jefe dice que él *prefiere* el turno noche, ¿pueden creer?

"Yes, the new guy," Amalia answers. "The boss says he prefers the night shift, can you believe?"

—Bueno, no es tan extraño —contesta Francisco—. Pagan más que durante el día; por eso estamos aquí.

"Well, it's not that strange," Francisco answers. "They pay more than during the day; that's why we are here."

—Ok, puede ser —responde Amalia—. Pero él *es* un poco raro, ¿no es cierto?

"Okay, it could be," Amalia answers. "But he's a bit weird, isn't he?"

Francisco se reclina sobre la silla para pensar.

Francisco leans back in his chair to think.

—Es cierto que elige siempre el escritorio del fondo —dice Francisco—. El más oscuro, y el que está más lejos de las ventanas. ¿Quién hace eso?

"It's true that he always chooses the desk in the back," says Francisco. "The one in the dark, and the furthest from the windows. Who does that?".

—No lo sé —responde Jésica—. Quizás tiene que ver con que es muy pálido.

"I don't know," says Jessica. "Maybe it has to do with being very pale."

—¿Dices que está enfermo, o algo así? —pregunta Francisco.

"Are you saying he's ill, or something?" asks Francisco.

Amalia mira el gran espejo. Se ve a sí misma, conversando con sus colegas, y se acomoda el cabello.

Amalia looks at the big mirror. She sees herself, chatting with her colleagues, and she fixes her hair.

—¡Por supuesto que Vladimir está enfermo! —exclama Amalia—. Si nunca come. Trabaja aquí desde hace cinco días, y no lo vi comer ni una vez.

"Of course Vladimir is ill!" Amalia exclaims. "He never eats. He has been working here for five days, and I never saw him eat once."

—Quizás come antes de venir... —insinúa Francisco.

"Maybe he eats before coming here..." Francisco suggests.

—Hacemos turnos de ocho horas —responde Amalia—. Hay que comer *algo*. Y él solo bebe ese repugnante jugo rojo que guarda en la heladera. ¿Qué es, kombucha?

"We do eight-hour shifts," Amalia answers. "You have to eat something. And he only drinks that nasty red juice that he keeps in the fridge. What is it, kombucha?"

—No sé, pero nunca se levanta de su silla —responde Francisco—. Seguramente va a ser el próximo empleado del mes.

"I don't know, but he never gets up from his chair," Francisco answers. "He surely is going to be the next employee of the month."

—Igualmente es muy amable —dice Jésica.

"In any case, he's also very kind," says Jessica.

—Es verdad —responde Francisco—. Tiene los modales de un duque.

"It's true," Francisco answers. "He has the manners of a duke."

—Salvo el otro día, frente a la impresora —agrega Jésica—. ¡Su expresión ante un corte de papel! Parece ser muy impresionable.

"Except the other day, in front of the printer," Jésica adds. "His face after he saw a paper cut! He seems to be very impressionable."

—Espera un segundo… —dice Amalia—. Quizás es una locura, pero, ¿Qué tal si…?

"Wait a second…" Amalia says. "Maybe this is crazy, but what if…?"

—Permiso —interrumpe una voz grave desde la puerta.

"Excuse me," interrupts a deep voice from the door.

Amalia, Francisco y Jésica se sobresaltan al escuchar la voz de Vladimir. Sus pasos son muy silenciosos: nunca nadie lo oye llegar.

Amalia, Francisco and Jésica jump when they hear Vladimir's voice. His steps are very silent: nobody ever hears him coming.

Vladimir entra en la sala de descanso y abre el refrigerador. Saca una botella de vidrio con un líquido rojo y bebe un trago. Unas gotas se derraman y le manchan la camisa blanca, casi tan blanca como él.

Vladimir walks into the break room and opens the fridge. He takes out a glass bottle filled with red liquid and takes a drink. A few drops spill and stain his white shirt, almost as white as he is.

—¡Maldición, era nueva! —dice, y luego, volviéndose a sus compañeros y ofreciendo la botella, agrega—: ¿Quieren?

"Damn it, it was new!" he says, and then, turning to his companions and offering the bottle, he adds, "Do you want some?"

Amalia, Francisco y Jésica se miran con inquietud. Todos saben lo que el otro está pensando.

Amalia, Francisco and Jésica exchange an uneasy look. They all know what the rest is thinking.

—Por favor —dice Amalia finalmente.

"Please," Amalia says finally.

Vladimir sirve su bebida en el vaso de Amalia. Y ella, lentamente, da un trago.

Vladimir pours his drink into Amalia's glass. And she slowly takes a drink.

—¿Gazpacho? —pregunta Amalia.

"Gazpacho?" Amalia asks.

—Últimamente no puedo comer otra cosa, estoy *fascinado* desde mi viaje a España —responde Vladimir.

"I can't eat anything else, lately, I'm fascinated since my trip to Spain," says Vladimir.

Amalia, Francisco y Jésica suspiran y sonríen. Vladimir, mientras tanto, ve a sus tres compañeros reflejados en el espejo, junto a una botella de gazpacho que flota en el aire.

Amalia, Francisco and Jésica sigh and smile. Vladimir, meanwhile, sees his three companions reflected in the mirror, next to a bottle of gazpacho that floats in the air.

Chapter 19 - Negative Sentences

No matter how positive you are in life, sometimes you need to say *no*!

Fortunately, forming negative sentences in Spanish is quite simple. If you simply add the word "no" to an affirmative sentence, it becomes negative (not that in English it's not as straightforward).

For example:

Yo tengo un automóvil - I have a car

Yo no tengo un automóvil - I don't have a car

But *no* is not the only word you need to know. These are the basic words you will need to form negative sentences:

no is no.

nada is nothing.

nadie is nobody.

nunca or *jamás* is never.

nungún, *ninguno* or *ninguna* is none.

tampoco is neither-

ni is nor.

ya no is not anymore.

ni siquiera is not even.

Learn how to use negative sentences with these 50 examples:

***No* - No**

David no tiene una bicicleta - David does not have a bike

No me gusta la pasta - I don't like pasta

Martina no está aquí - Martina is not here

No tengo mascotas - I do not have pets

¡Claro que no! - Of course not!

No lo conozco - I don't know him

No podéis sentaros allí - You can't sit there

No he estudiado - I have not studied

No sé nada - I know nothing

No me interesan los videojuegos - I'm not interested in video games

***Nada* - Nothing**

Allí no hay nada - There's nothing there

¿No tienes nada nuevo para contarme? - Don't you have anything new to tell me?

Fui a la tienda, pero no tenían nada - I went to the store but they had nothing

No tengo nada de frío - I'm not cold at all

Sin mis anteojos, no veo casi nada - Without my glasses, I see almost nothing

No tengo nada de efectivo - I have no cash at all

No tienes nada que perder - You have nothing to lose

Eso no tiene nada que ver - That has nothing to do with it

¿No viste nada sospechoso? - Didn't you see anything suspicious?

No ha quedado nada de comida - There is no food left

***Nadie* - Nobody**

¿Nadie te ayudó? - Nobody helped you?

No hay nadie - There is nobody

Nadie sospecha de ella - No one suspects her

Nadie fue al evento - No one went to the event

Nadie vio a Juan - Nobody saw Juan

Nadie es perfecto - Nobody is perfect

Nadie se dio cuenta - Nobody noticed

Nadie te conoce mejor que Teresa - Nobody knows you better than Teresa

No dejes que nadie se acerque - Don't let anyone near it

¿Todavía no llegó nadie? - Hasn't anyone arrived yet?

Nunca - Never

Nunca vi un lugar así - I've never seen such a place like this

Nunca me visitas - You never visit me

Pedro nunca cocina - Pedro never cooks

Nunca más digas eso - Never say that again

Vosotros nunca me tomáis en serio - You never take me seriously

¿Tú nunca desayunas? - Do you never eat breakfast?

Nunca vi un oso - I have never seen a bear

Nunca me sentí mejor - I've never felt better

Miguel nunca llega a tiempo - Miguel is never on time

Rosa nunca come verduras - Rosa never eats vegetables

Ningún, ninguno

Ninguno de nosotros sabe conducir - None of us knows how to drive

Ninguno de ellos es perfecto - None of them are perfect

No tengo ninguna duda - I have no doubts

¡De ninguna manera! - No way!

Ningún supermercado está abierto ahora - Not one supermarket is open now

Otras expresiones

A mí tampoco - Me neither

Jamás vienes por aquí - You never come around here

No han venido ni Felipe ni Cristina - Neither Felipe nor Cristina have come

Ya no te creo - I do not believe you anymore

Carmen ni siquiera me llamó para mi cumpleaños - Carmen didn't even call me for my birthday

Chapter 20 - Forming Questions (part I)

Do you like learning Spanish? Have you learned a lot so far? Will you learn much more in the ten remaining chapters?

To answer all these questions, first you have to be able to form them, right? In this first chapter dedicated to questions, we will learn how to form and ask closed questions; that is, 'yes or no' questions. We will learn how to form questions using *what, where, when, why and how* in chapter 22.

To form 'yes or no' questions in Spanish in writing, you simply need to add question marks to an affirmative sentence. In the oral speech, you need to change the intonation for people to understand it's a question. That's it! You don't need to move around the parts of the sentence, as in English. For example:

Tienes mucha hambre - You're very hungry

¿Tienes mucha hambre? - Are you very hungry?

In writing, note that in Spanish we have not one but *two* question marks, one at the beginning and one at the end of the question. The opening question mark looks like the closing question mark but upside down.

You *must* use this opening question mark in formal writing (for example, in a work-related document, in a paper or a university assignment). If you're writing in an informal context (i.e., a text message), don't worry about it; the closing question is just fine.

Now, listen to 50 practical examples of Spanish 'yes or no' questions:

Familia - Family

¿Eres hijo único? - Are you an only child?

¿Vives con tus padres? - Do you live with your parents?

¿Tu hermano compró pan? - Did your brother buy bread?

¿Tus padres son médicos? - Are your parents doctors?

¿Tienes muchos hermanos? - Do you have many siblings?

¿Te fuiste de vacaciones con tus padres? - Did you go on vacation with your parents?

¿El abuelo vendrá? - Will grandpa come?

¿Tu familia es muy grande? - Is your family very large?

¿La casa es de tus abuelos? - Do your grandparents own the house?

¿Ustedes cenan en familia? - Do you have dinner together as a family?

Trabajo y estudios - Work and study

¿Él es profesor? - Is he a teacher?

¿Terminaste de estudiar? - Did you finish studying?

¿Quieres ir a la universidad? - Do you want to go to university?

¿Vas a trabajar? - Are you going to work?

¿Tu padre vive cerca de su oficina? - Does your father live near his office?

¿Fuiste a la escuela ayer? - Did you go to school yesterday?

¿Ella es tu médica? - Is she your doctor?

¿Te han dado un teléfono corporativo? - Have you been given a corporate phone?

¿Aprobaste el examen? - Did you pass the test?

¿Le avisaste a tu jefe que no irás mañana? - Did you tell your boss that you are not going tomorrow?

Objetos - Objects

¿Estás usando ese lápiz? - Are you using that pencil?

¿Tu computadora es lenta? - Is your computer slow?

¿El té está caliente? - Is the tea hot?

¿Puedo tomaros una foto? - Can I take a picture of you?

¿Sabes si esa tienda está abierta? - Do you know if that store is open?

¿Tienes repelente? - Do you have bug repellent?

¿Llevas un bolso? - Are you taking a bag with you?

¿Me sirve un café, por favor? - Can I have a coffee, please?

¿Tienes dinero? - Do you have money?

¿Tu apartamento tiene vista al mar? - Does your apartment have an ocean view?

Relaciones - Relationships

¿Él tiene muchos amigos? - Does he have many friends?

¿Vas a venir con tu esposa? - Are you coming with your wife?

¿Estamos invitados a la boda? - Are we invited to the wedding?

¿Te fuiste de vacaciones con tus amigos? - Did you go on vacation with your friends?

¿Mi amiga está aquí? - Is my friend here?

¿Vosotros dos sois colegas? - Are you two colleagues?

¿Disfrutaste la cena con tu amiga? - Did you enjoy having dinner with your friend?

¿Él es tu socio? - Is he your partner?

¿Tenemos que ir a la fiesta de cumpleaños? - Do we have to go to the birthday party?

¿Conoces a mi novio? - Have you met my boyfriend?

Gustos y opiniones

¿Te gustan las películas de superhéroes? - Do you like superhero movies?

¿A vos también te encanta el helado? - Do you also love ice cream?

¿Te parece que mi casa es grande? - Do you think my house is big?

¿Me veo bien? - Do I look good?

¿Tienes miedo? - Are you afraid?

¿Prefieres la playa o la montaña? - Do you prefer the beach or the mountain?

¿La pizza está fría? - Is the pizza cold?

¿No te gusta el chocolate? - You don't like chocolate?

¿Crees que debería estudiar más? - Do you think I should study more?

¿Piensas que debería dejarme el pelo largo? - Do you think I should grow my hair long?

Chapter 21 - Formal and Informal Speech

As you might remember from chapter 5, "Personal pronouns", in Spanish we have six different words for "you". Yes, six!

There are the plural versions of "you": "vosotros" and "vosotras" (used in Spain) and "ustedes" (used in Latin America).

We also have the singular versions of "you". In most countries, we use "tú", but in some countries (such as Argentina, Uruguay, Paraguay and some regions in other countries) we use "vos".

And, finally, we have the *formal* singular "you": *usted*.

Usted is how you would address a person in a formal context, either in Latin America or Spain. Verbs for this pronoun are always conjugated as the third singular person (he/she). For example:

Tu sabes mucho - You know a lot

Usted sabe mucho - You know a lot

There are no strict rules on when to use *usted* instead of *tú* or *vos*; some cultures are more formal and some others are more informal.

In general, we would recommend you to use formal speech in these situations:

- Talking to a stranger.
- Talking to an older person.
- Talking to your boss.
- Talking to a professor.
- Talking to an 'important' person (of course, we're all important, but you know what we mean!)

You can generally use informal speech with people you age, even if you don't know them. If in doubt, you can always ask people if you can treat them informally, like this: "*¿Puedo tutearte?*".

Practice formal and informal speech with this short story:

El niño perdido - The lost boy

Federico mira a su alrededor y solo ve bosque. Los árboles son muy altos. Es de día, pero falta poco para la noche. La temperatura está bajando. Y Federico está solo.

Federico looks around and sees only forest. The trees are very tall. It is daytime, but the night is just a short time away. The temperature is dropping. And Federico is alone.

—¿Qué haces aquí? —pregunta una voz—. ¿Estás perdido?

"What are you doing here?" someone asks. "Are you lost?"

Federico se voltea. Ve entonces a una mujer mayor, de la edad de su abuela. Tiene el pelo blanco muy corto, shorts marrones y zapatillas para caminar. Carga una mochila negra que parece pesada, y lo mira con preocupación.

Federico turns around. He then sees an old woman, about the age of his grandmother. She has short white hair, brown shorts, and walking shoes. She carries a heavy-looking black backpack, and she looks at him with concern.

—¿Cómo te llamas? —pregunta la mujer.

"What's your name?" the woman asks.

—Mi nombre es Federico —contesta Federico finalmente—. ¿Cuál es su nombre?

"My name is Federico," Federico finally answers. "What is your name?"

—Alicia —responde la mujer—. Escúchame, ¿dónde está tu mamá?

"Alicia," the woman replies. "Listen to me, where is your mom?"

—Está más atrás —dice Federico—. O más adelante. O... No sé. ¿Quizás usted la conoce? Mi mamá se llama Silvia.

"She's behind," says Federico. "Or maybe ahead. Or... I don't know. Maybe you know her? My mom's name is Silvia.

La voz de Federico tiembla; sin embargo, no llora.

Federico's voice trembles; however, he does not cry.

—No conozco a tu mamá —dice Alicia—. Pero creo que sé dónde puede estar. Hay un refugio a unos minutos hacia el norte. Ven conmigo, te llevo.

"I don't know your mom," Alicia says. "But I think I know where she can be. There is a shelter a few minutes to the north. Come with me, I'll take you."

—Disculpe, pero mi mamá dice que no debo irme con desconocidos —responde Federico.

"I'm sorry, but my mom says I shouldn't go with strangers," Federico replies.

Alicia piensa un segundo. Entonces saca una brújula de su bolsillo y se la enseña a Federico.

Alicia thinks for a second. She then takes out a compass from her pocket and shows it to Federico.

—¿Sabes qué es esto? —pregunta Alicia.

"Do you know what this is?" Alicia asks.

Federico dice que no con la cabeza.

Federico shakes his head.

—Es una brújula —continúa Alicia—. Los aventureros, los piratas y los vaqueros la usan para orientarse. Mira, esta flecha apunta hacia el norte, en dirección al refugio. Podemos ir ambos hacia allí. De esta forma tú no me sigues: vamos juntos.

"It's a compass," Alicia continues. "Adventurers, pirates, and cowboys use it to know where they are. Look, this arrow is pointing north, towards the shelter. We can both go there. In this way you are not going with me: we are simply both going there at the same time."

—Supongo que eso está bien —responde Federico—. ¿Me puede prestar la brújula?

"I guess that's okay," Federico answers. "Can you lend me the compass?"

Alicia le da la brújula al niño. Ambos caminan unos minutos por el sendero; ya casi es de noche. Finalmente, encuentran una gran casa de madera, de donde sale un humo acogedor.

Alice gives the compass to the boy. They both walk for a few minutes on the path; it is almost night. Finally, they find a large wooden house, from which a cozy smoke comes out.

—¿Esa es tu mamá? —pregunta Alicia, señalando a una mujer alta que espera de pie frente al refugio.

"Is that your mom?" Alicia asks, pointing to a tall woman standing in front of the shelter.

—¡Sí! —responde Federico. Le devuelve la brújula a Alicia y sale corriendo hacia su madre.

"Yes!" Federico replies. He returns the compass to Alicia and runs towards his mom.

—¡Federico! —grita la madre, abrazándolo—. ¡Me asusté! ¿Dónde estabas?

"Federico!" shouts the mother, hugging him. "I was afraid! Where were you?"

—Me perdí —dice el niño—. Pero esa señora me ayudó.

"I got lost," says the boy. "But that lady helped me."

—Muchas gracias, señora —dice la madre de Federico—. ¿Desea comer con nosotros?

"Thank you very much, ma'am," says Federico's mother. "Do you want to eat with us?"

—No gracias, querida —dice Alicia—. Voy a volver a mi tienda de campaña ahora… Pero antes, Federico, toma esta brújula. Quédatela. Te servirá para encontrar tu camino."

"No thanks, dear," says Alicia. "I'm going back to my tent now… But first, Federico, take this compass. Keep it. It will help find your way."

Chapter 22 - Forming Questions (part II)

As we anticipated in chapter 20, the first of two dedicated to forming and asking questions, we are now going to learn how to make questions using *what, when, where, why, how, how much* and *which?*

These are the basic words you need to know to ask open questions in Spanish:

qué is what.

quién is who.

quiénes is plural who.

cuándo is when.

dónde is where.

por qué is why.

cómo is how.

cuánto is how much.

cuántos is how many.

cuál is which one.

cuáles is which ones.

Now, listen to fifty practical examples of these question words to learn how to use them:

¿Qué? - What?

¿Qué estudias? - What do you study?

¿Qué hacéis? - What are you doing?

¿Qué quiere tu perro? - What does your dog want?

¿Qué buscas? - What are you looking for?

¿Qué hacemos mañana? - What do we do tomorrow?

¿Qué te pasa? - What's wrong?

¿Quién? / ¿Quiénes? - Who?

¿Quién se comió mi postre? - Who ate my dessert?

¿Quién es ella? - Who is she?

¿Quién anda ahí? - Who's there?

¿Quién sabe la respuesta? - Who knows the answer?

¿Quién quiere helado? - Who wants ice cream?

¿Quiénes van a venir a nuestra boda? - Who will come to our wedding?

¿Quiénes son ellos? - Who are they?

¿Cuándo? - **When?**

¿Cuándo vas a volver? - When are you coming back?

¿Cuándo fue la última vez que viajaste? - When was the last time you traveled?

¿Cuándo vamos a la playa? - When are we going to the beach?

¿Cuándo nació? - When was he born?

¿Cuándo voy a conocer a tus padres? - When am I going to meet your parents?

¿Cuándo lo supiste? - When did you know?

¿Dónde? - **Where?**

¿Dónde estás? - Where are you?

¿Dónde están mis zapatos? - Where are my shoes?

¿De dónde sos? - Where are you from?

¿Dónde nació tu abuela? - Where was your grandmother born?

¿Por dónde salgo? - Which way is the exit?

¿Dónde está tu pueblo? - Where is your town?

¿Dónde quieres ir? - Where do you want to go?

¿Por qué? - **Why?**

¿Por qué te mudaste aquí? - Why did you move here?

¿Por qué siempre me pasan estas cosas? - Why do these things always happen to me?

¿Por qué no viniste? - Why didn't you come?

¿Por qué hablas así? - Why do you like that?

¿Por qué Claudia es tan molesta? - Why is Claudia so annoying?

¿Por qué no nos vamos? - Why don't we leave?

¿Cómo? - How?

¿Cómo estás? - How are you?

¿Cómo dijiste? - What did you say?

¿Cómo hicieron para llegar tan rápido? - How did you get here so fast?

¿Cómo resuelvo este problema? - How do I solve this problem?

¿Cómo quieres tu café? - How do you want your coffee?

¿Cómo se llama tu mascota? - What is your pet's name?

¿Cuánto? / ¿Cuántos? - How much? / How many?

¿Cuántas mascotas tienes? - How many pets do you have?

¿Cuánto pagaste por eso? - How much did you pay for that?

¿Cuántas veces te lo dije? - How many times did I tell you?

¿Cuánto hace que os conocéis? - How long have you known each other?

¿Cuánto mide este edificio? - How tall is this building?

¿Cuánto disfrutaste tu cumpleaños? - How much did you enjoy your birthday?

¿Cuál? / ¿Cuáles? - Which one? / Which ones?

¿Cuál es tu sabor de helado favorito? - What is your favourite ice cream flavor?

¿Cuáles son tus aptitudes? - What skills do you have?

¿Cuál es tu objetivo? - What is your goal?

¿Cuál es el motivo por el que llegas tarde? - What's the reason you are late?

¿Cuál es tu automóvil? - Which one is your car?

¿Cuáles son tus amigos? - Which ones are your friends?

Chapter 23 - Telling the Time

We've learned the Spanish numbers in chapter 7. Now, let's put them to a practical use. In this chapter, we will explain how to read and tell the time.

To tell the hour, we use the verb "ser" conjugated in the third person of the present tense. For 1 a. m. or 1 p. m., we use the singular conjugation "es"; for the rest of the time, we use plural conjugation "son". Next, we add the feminine definite articles "la" or "las". Finally, we add "de la mañana" (in the morning), "de la tarde" (in the afternoon) or "de la noche" (at night).

These are the hours of the early morning and the morning:

It's 1 a. m. - *es la una de la mañana.*

It's 2 a. m. - *son las dos de la mañana.*

It's 3 a. m. - *son las tres de la mañana.*

It's 4 a. m. - *son las cuatro de la mañana.*

It's 5 a. m. - *son las cinco de la mañana.*

It's 6 a. m. - *son las seis de la mañana.*

It's 7 a. m. - *son las siete de la mañana.*

It's 8 a. m. - *son las ocho de la mañana.*

It's 9 a. m. - *son las nueve de la mañana.*

It's 10 a. m. - *son las diez de la mañana.*

It's 11 a. m. - *son las once de la mañana.*

The noon is called "mediodía". If you're asked what time is it at noon, you can say: "son las doce del mediodía". Some people will also include 1 p. m. within the "noon" hours: "es la una del mediodía"

These are the hours of the afternoon:

It's 1 p. m. - *es la una de la tarde*

It's 2 p. m. - *son las dos de la tarde*

It's 3 p. m. - *son las tres de la tarde*

It's 4 p. m. - *son las cuatro de la tarde*

It's 5 p. m. - *son las cinco de la tarde*

It's 6 p. m. - *son las seis de la tarde*

It's 7 p. m. - *son las siete de la tarde*

Whether 7 p. m. is "afternoon" or "night" will depend on the region you're visiting and the time of the year. But in most cases, 6 p. m. will be considered part of the afternoon and 8 p. m. part of the nighttime.

These are the hours of the night:

It's 7 p. m. - *son las siete de la noche*

It's 8 p. m. - *son las ocho de la noche*

It's 9 p. m. - *son las nueve de la noche*

It's 10 p. m. - *son las diez de la noche*

It's 11 p. m. - *son las once de la noche*

Midnight is called "medianoche". To tell the time at midnight, you can say "Son las doce de la noche" or "Es medianoche".

Learn more time-related vocabulary with these 50 example sentences:

Preguntas - Questions

¿Qué hora es? - What time is it?

¿Tienes hora? - Do you have the time?

¿Puedes decirme la hora? - Can you tell me what the time is?

¿A qué hora nos encontramos? - What time do we meet?

¿Cuánto falta para las cinco? - How long until five?

¿Cuánto falta para la comida? - How much longer is lunch going to be?

¿Falta mucho para las seis? - Is it long before six?

¿Ya son las siete? - Is it seven already?

¿A qué hora sale el tren? - What time does the train leave?

¿Puedes recogerme a las once? - Can you pick me up at eleven?

Horarios - Times

En esta casa almorzamos a la una en punto - In this house we have lunch at one o'clock

Es la una y diez - It's ten past one

Es la una y quince - It's one-fifteen

Son las dos y cuarto - It's quarter past two

Son las dos y media - It's half past two

Son las tres menos veinte - It's twenty to three

Son las cinco y veinticinco - It is five twenty-five

Son las cinco y treinta - It's five thirty

Son las cinco y treinta y cinco - It's five thirty-five

Aquí siempre cenamos en a eso de las siete - Here we always have dinner at around seven

Ya son pasadas las ocho - It's already past eight

Van a ser las nueve - Soon it'll be nine o'clock

Pasaron seis minutos de las nueve - It's six minutes past nine

Apenas pasaron unos minutos de las diez - It's barely a few minutes past ten

A las diez de la noche van a emitir mi programa favorito - At ten o'clock at night my favorite program is broadcasted

Faltan ocho minutos para las once - It's eight minutes to eleven

En cinco minutos, el autobús pasará a recogernos - In five minutes, the bus will pick us up

Momentos del día - Moments of the day

El alba es preciosa - Dawn is beautiful

Me encanta desayunar al amanecer - I love having breakfast at dawn

Mi padre lee el periódico por la mañana - My father reads the newspaper in the morning

A media mañana, tomo un yogur - I have a yogurt in the mid-morning

Hace mucho calor al mediodía - It's very hot at noon

Fernanda toma una siesta a media tarde - Fernanda takes a nap in the mid-afternoon

Voy a ir al supermercado esta tarde - I'm going to the supermarket this afternoon

La temperatura desciende después del atardecer - Temperature drops after sunset

El atardecer es hermoso - The sunset is beautiful

Mañana a la noche festejo mi cumpleaños - Tomorrow night I will celebrate my birthday

Son las doce de la noche - It's midnight

Ya es medianoche - It's already midnight

En la madrugada, todo el mundo duerme - During the early morning everyone is asleep

Vocabulario relacionado - Related vocab

Todavía es muy temprano - It is still too early

Es momento de prepararse para ir a trabajar - It's time to get ready to go to work

Si no nos apuramos, vamos a llegar tarde - If we don't hurry, we'll be late

No tengo tiempo para nada - I do not have time for anything

Falta poco para la una - It's not long before one o'clock

No falta mucho para que empiece el espectáculo - It won't be long before the show starts

Creo que tienes demasiado tiempo libre - I think you have too much free time

¿Tu reloj es analógico o digital? - Is your watch analog or digital?

Martín suele ser impuntual - Martín is usually unpunctual

Carla es muy puntual - Carla is very punctual

Chapter 24 - Adverbs

Adverbs are those words that usually describe verbs. Adverbs that end in *-ly* in English normally end in *-mente* in Spanish.

For example:

Marcos come rápidamente - Marcos eats quickly

Me mudé aquí recientemente - I moved here recently

Habla lentamente, por favor - Speak slowly, please

Just as in English there are adverbs that don't end in *-ly*, in Spanish there are some adverbs that don't end in *-mente*:

lento - slow

rápido - fast

así - like this

bien - well

mal - wrong

There are adverbs that indicate location, time, space, mode, quantity, and there are "epistemic" adverbs, such as *sí* (yes), *no* (no), *nunca* (never) and *también* (also), which you've learned in other chapters.

Listen and practice Spanish adverbs with this fun short story. Can you identify them all? Also, since you've already reached chapter 24 and you're getting near the end of this audiobook, we have a new challenge... Short stories from now on will be only in Spanish.

To help you out a little bit, we'll include some vocab at the end.

Los gatos del barrio - *The cats from the neighborhood*

Hoy es el día en que Juan, el carnicero, recibe su nueva mercadería.

Por eso, los gatos Manchita y Toto esperan en la esquina del local.

Manchita se echa bajo el sol y lame su pata delicadamente. Es una gata muy peluda, y tiene un ojo azul y uno marrón. Mientras tanto, Toto da vueltas a su alrededor.

—Hoy es el día —dice Toto, alegremente.

—Así es —responde Manchita, tranquilamente.

—Estoy un poco ansioso, ¿sabes? —continúa Toto.

Manchita abre apenas su ojo azul.

—¡Es evidente! —dice Manchita.

—Creo que la mejor forma de robar la carne es entrar rápidamente al camión repartidor —propone Toto—. Después hay que morder algún trozo y huir velozmente.

—Puede ser —responde Manchita, perezosamente—. ¿Tú puedes cargar mucha carne?

—No demasiada... —dice Toto.

—Ya veo —contesta Manchita.

—Pero esa es la mejor forma —responde Toto—. Algunos dicen que conviene entrar en la carnicería por la noche... Entrar sigilosamente y comer toda la carne posible. No me parece mal, pero creo que es muy difícil.

—Realmente no suena sencillo —dice Manchita, entre bostezos.

—¡Mira, ahí viene! —exclama Toto súbitamente, y empieza a correr.

Toto se mueve ágilmente, y consigue morder un pequeño trozo de carne caído en el suelo. Logra llevarlo de vuelta al rincón donde espera Manchita.

Toto está agitado y tenso, pero se siente alegre por su triunfo. Ni Juan ni los empleados del camión lo vieron.

—¿Lo has visto? —pregunta Toto—. Estuve increíblemente cerca.

—Sí, sí —contesta Manchita, desinteresada, mientras se levanta—. Eres genial...

Entonces, Manchita se acerca a la puerta de la carnicería, se sienta sobre sus patas traseras y comienza a maullar lastimeramente. Es un canto triste y desolador. Juan, el carnicero, mira apenado los ojos de dos colores de la gata.

—¡Oigan, chicos! —exclama el carnicero Juan firmamente—. No olviden dejar un buen trozo de carne para la gatita, ¿de acuerdo?

Vocab:

carnicero is butcher.

carne is meat.

gato is cat.

robar is to steal.

camión is truck.

bostezo is yawning.

suelo is floor.

maullar is to meow.

trozo is chunk.

Now, go back and listen to the story one more time!

Chapter 25 - Present continuous

Just as in English, in Spanish we have our version of present continuous to talk about what is happening right now.

Just as in English, we form this present continuous with the present tense conjugation of verb *estar* (to be) + the gerund of the action verb.

Gerunds of regular verbs in Spanish are formed like this:

For -ar verbs, you lose the *-ar* ending and add *-ando*.

For -er and *-ir* verbs, you lose the ending and add *-iendo*.

The gerund of *cantar* (to sing) is *cantando* (singing).

The gerund of *beber* (to drink) is *bebiendo* (drinking).

The gerund of *vivir* (to live) is *viviendo* (living).

If we put this together with the verb estar, we have the present continuous. For example:

Estoy cantando con mis amigas (I'm singing with my friends).

Juan está bebiendo agua (Juan is drinking water).

Laura está viviendo en Alemania (Laura is living in Germany).

Practice the present continuous with these 50 example sentences:

Modo afirmativo - Affirmative mode

Estoy jugando al básquet - I'm playing basketball

Estoy cantando bajo la lluvia - I'm singing in the rain

Estoy trabajando - I'm working

Lo que estás diciendo es muy bonito - What you are saying is very nice

¡Estás haciendo un gran esfuerzo! - You're making a great effort!

Lucas está durmiendo - Lucas is sleeping

Agustina está usando un vestido - Agustina is wearing a dress

Estamos disfrutando esta fiesta - We are enjoying this party

Estamos viendo una película - We are watching a movie

Estamos yendo al parque - We are going to the park

Estamos comiendo pasta - We are eating pasta

Ustedes están ayudándome mucho - You are helping me a lot

Los niños están merendando - The children are having a snack

Los gatos están maullando - The cats are meowing

Úrsula y Juan están corriendo una maratón - Úrsula y Juan are running a marathon

Modo negativo - Negative mode

No estoy leyendo un libro - I am not reading a book

No estoy comiendo verduras - I'm not eating vegetables

No estoy yendo al gimnasio - I'm not going to the gym

No me está gustando mucho este videojuego - I'm not really liking this video game

Creo que no estoy entendiendo la lección - I think I'm not understanding the lesson

No estás prestando atención - You're not paying attention

No estoy viendo televisión - I'm not watching television

Vos no estás tomando café - You're not drinking coffee

Marcos no está usando su gorra nueva - Marcos is not wearing his new cap

Cristina no está nadando - Cristina is not swimming

Ella no está viniendo todavía - She's not coming yet

Mi perro no está comiendo mucho - My dog isn't eating a lot

No nos estamos viendo muy seguido - We are not seeing each other very often

No estamos bailando - We are not dancing

Ustedes no están viviendo en esta ciudad, ¿no? - You are not living in this city, are you?

Modo interrogativo - Interrogative mode

¿Te estoy molestando? - I'm bothering you?

¿Estoy siendo claro? - Am I being clear?

¿Estás estudiando? - Are you studying?

¿Cómo estás durmiendo? - How are you sleeping?

¿Te estás divirtiendo? - Are you having fun?

¿Estás sintiéndote bien? - Are you feeling well?

¿Me estás tomando el pelo? - Are you kidding me?

¿Estás siguiendo las instrucciones? - Are you following the instructions?

¿Estás bebiendo algo? - Are you drinking something?

¿Estás escuchando música? - Are you listening to music?

¿Estás viendo eso? - Are you seeing that?

¿Crees que Gabriel está mintiendo? - Do you think Gabriel is lying?

¿Me estás oyendo? - Are you listening to me?

¿Rubén está llegando? - Is Rubén arriving?

¿Benjamín está pintando? - Is Benjamín painting?

¿Qué estáis haciendo aquí? - What are you doing here?

¿Ya estáis viniendo? - Are you already coming?

¿Están usando el microondas? - Are you using the microwave?

¿Los gatos están comiendo? - Are the cats eating?

¿María y Pedro están saliendo? - Are María and Pedro dating?

Chapter 26 - Prepositions (part I)

Spanish prepositions can be a challenge for non-natives. There are 19 common prepositions and we've divided them into two chapters to make things easier for you. In this chapter, we'll learn the easiest 9 of them: *a, con, de, desde, en, hacia, hasta, sin, sobre.*

Most of these can be translated as many English prepositions, since they're not used in exactly the same way. These are the most common translations:

a is *to*.

con is *with*.

de is *from* or *of*.

desde is *from* or *since*.

en is *in, on, at, into, inside*

hacia is *towards, to*.

hasta is *until, up to*.

sin is *without*.

sobre is *on, over, about*.

Practice these prepositions with 50 practical sentences:

a - to

Viajo a Barcelona - I travel to Barcelona

Andrea visita a Pedro - Andrea visits Pedro

Las clases comienzan a las ocho - Classes start at eight

Yo amo a mis hermanos - I love my siblings

Ven a comer - Come to eat

El supermercado está a la derecha - The supermarket is to the right

con - with

Voy a una fiesta con mis amigos - I go to a party with my friends

El perro mueve la cola con alegría - The dog wags his tail with joy

¿Quieres un café con leche? - Do you want a coffee with milk?

Tengo una casa con parque - I have a house with a garden

Esta es la computadora con la que trabajo - This is the computer I work with

Gabriel y Rosa están con un resfrío - Gabriel and Rosa have a cold

de - of, from

Este suéter es de lana - This sweater is made of wool

El gato de Luis es gruñón - Luis's cat is grumpy

Me gusta la leche de almendras - I like almond milk

Laura viene de Alemania - Laura comes from Germany

Este es un libro de mi autora favorita - This is a book by my favorite author

¿Vamos a la casa de tus padres? - Are we going to your parents' house?

desde - from, since

Voy desde mi casa a la escuela - I go from my house to school

No he visto a mi abuelo desde Navidad - I haven't seen my grandfather since Christmas

Te estoy buscando desde hace un rato - I've been looking for you for a while

¿Desde cuándo te gusta la cerveza? - Since when do you like beer?

Él va en metro desde su casa hasta el trabajo - He goes by metro from his house to work

en - in, on, at, into, inside

Hay lechuzas en ese bosque - There are owls in that forest

Martín y Laura están en la universidad - Martín and Laura are at college

Tu camisa está en la mesa - Your shirt is on the table

Puse tus zapatos en el armario - I put your shoes into the closet

Mi hermana vive en Chile - My sister lives in Chile

hacia - towards, to

Lucas camina hacia el tren - Lucas walks towards the train

Tengo un gran amor hacia los gatos - I have a great love towards cats

Viajo hacia el sur - I'm travelling to the south

Voy hacia allá - I'm going over there

Voy a llegar hacia las cinco - I'm going to arrive around five

hasta - until, up to

Dormí hasta las diez - I slept up until ten

Voy solo hasta la esquina - I only go up to the corner

Laura camina hasta el supermercado - Laura walks to the supermarket

Todavía hay tiempo hasta que venga el autobús - There's still time until the bus comes

¡Hasta pronto! - See you soon!

sin - without

Me gusta el café sin azúcar - I like coffee without sugar

Debo resolver el examen sin calculadora - I have to solve the exam without a calculator

Pasó mucho tiempo sin lluvia - There's been a long time without rain

No vayas sin desayunar - Don't go without having breakfast

A Paco le gustan las papas sin kétchup - Paco likes potatoes without ketchup

Sin dudas, Marta es inteligente - Without a doubt, Marta is smart

sobre - on, over, about

El perro está sobre el sofá - The dog is on the couch

El avión vuela sobre la ciudad - The plane flies over the city

Juan va a llegar sobre las nueve - Juan will arrive around nine

El loro está sobre el hombro del pirata - The parrot is on the pirate's shoulder

Este artículo trata sobre biología - This article is about biology

No sé mucho sobre ese tema - I don't know much about that topic

Chapter 27 - Food

Whether you're learning Spanish to move to Mexico, to go on an adventure to Spain or to go for work to South America, you should know that all across the Spanish-speaking world food is fundamental!

These are some of the traditional dishes you'll want to try in some of the largest Spanish speaking countries:

In **Spain**, you will want to try the *paella*, made with *arroz* (rice) and other ingredients. You can also enjoy the traditional *tapas*, small bites to eat on the go.

In **Mexico**, you will want to try *tacos* or *enchiladas*, two versions of corn *tortillas* topped with a filling.

In **Venezuela** or **Colombia**, try the *arepas*, made with ground maize dough.

In **Argentina**, eat *asado* (grilled meat).

And, in **Perú**, don't hesitate in trying the delicious *ceviche*, made with raw fish cured in lemon juice and spiced with chili peppers.

And, in practically all of Spain and Latin America, try different versions of *empanadas*, a baked turnover of pastry and with different fillings.

To drink, you can have a *cerveza* (beer) or *vino* (wine). If you don't want alcohol, you can always have *zumo de frutas* (fruit juice), *café* (coffee) or *un vaso de agua* (a glass of water).

Practice some more food-related vocab with this short story about a kitchen and an unwanted guest. Find some vocab at the end and listen as many times as you need until you understand the story!

La invitada indeseada - The unwanted guest

La cocina del restaurante El Español trabaja continuamente. Es un sótano grande y caluroso.

Hoy, todas las mesas están llenas. Los clientes eligen sus platos de un menú muy variado.

Hay especialidades españolas y argentinas, una variedad de comidas peruanas y hasta algún plato mexicano.

—¡¿Qué es eso?! —pregunta de pronto el ayudante de cocina. Su voz suena alterada—. Creo que es...

—¡¡Una rata!! —exclama el pastelero, mientras señala una rata gris que trepa por uno de los hornos.

El pastelero le arroja una espátula todavía recubierta de crema.

La rata, sin embargo, la evita y se esconde detrás de un palo de amasar. Luego, corre sobre la mesa donde reposan panes y pasteles. Sus pequeñas patas dejan huellas en las masas.

—¡Deténganla! —grita el ayudante de cocina, mientras le lanza lo que tiene a mano: una empanada de jamón y queso recién cocida. Pero la rata es muy ágil, y falla.

El chef de El Español decide tomar el asunto en sus propias manos. Toma un cuchillo amplio y filoso, y lo arroja en dirección a la invitada indeseada. Sin embargo, la rata consigue refugiarse dentro de una gran sartén con restos de una salsa bolognesa.

En ese momento, el lavacopas levanta la mirada de su trabajo y ve a todos sus compañeros arrojando ingredientes, comida y utensilios al roedor que corre por toda la cocina. Sin decir nada, toma una gran olla y se coloca en un rincón de la cocina.

A los pocos segundos, cuando la rata viene hacia él escapando de sus compañeros, se arroja al suelo con la olla hacia abajo, de forma que la rata queda atrapada dentro. Luego, desliza la tapa por debajo, levanta todo y sale de la cocina.

—¡Qué héroe! —dice el ayudante de cocina.

—¡El mejor! —grita el repostero.

—¡Un genio! —exclama el chef.

Una vez afuera, el lavacopas deja salir a la rata:

—Toma —le dice, dándole un trozo de queso que saca de su bolsillo—. Te he dicho mil veces que no entres en la cocina. Yo te daré tu queso, como siempre, pero debes esperar afuera.

La rata toma su queso, agradecida, y sale corriendo.

Vocab:

sótano is basement.

ayudante is assistant, aide.

pastelero is pastry chef, baker.

gris is gray.

horno is oven.

palo de amasar is *rolling pin*.

mesa is table.

pan is bread.

pastel is cake.

huella is footprint.

masa is dough.

jamón is ham.

queso is cheese.

cuchillo is knife.

sartén is pan.

lavacopas is dishwasher.

olla is pot.

Chapter 28 - Travelling (part I)

Congratulations!

You're getting to the end of this audiobook. And, since you know so many new things, we think it's time to start practicing travel-related vocabulary. You sure want to travel to Spain or Latin America, *¿verdad?*

We will be dedicating two full chapters to travel-related vocab. In this chapter, you will find 50 example sentences related to general tourism, travel-related objects, means of transportation, places and lodging.

In the last chapter of the book, chapter 30, we will give you some tips to travel around Latin America and Spain, and you will end by listening to our last short story, that takes place in an airport.

Let's start with the 50 example sentences...

***Turismo* - Tourism**

¡Comienzan las vacaciones! - The holidays begin!

Esa agencia de viajes es muy buena - That travel agency is very good

¿Dónde puedo alquilar un auto? - Where can I rent a car?

El centro histórico de la ciudad es precioso - The historic city center is beautiful

Me encanta ese monumento - I love that monument

Quiero hacer una excursión - I want to go on an excursion

Ese parque natural es muy grande - That natural park is very big

La plaza principal está en el centro de la ciudad - The main square is in the downtown

El museo tiene visitas guiadas - The museum has guided tours

Compré un paquete turístico - I bought a tour package

***Objetos* - Objects**

Este mapa es confuso - This map is confusing

Lucas lleva una maleta - Lucas carries a suitcase

¿Me permite su pasaporte? - May I have your passport?

Matías compra un pasaje - Matías buys a ticket

Esta es mi tarjeta de embarque - This is my boarding pass

Emanuel olvidó su tarjeta de crédito - Emanuel forgot his credit card

Estoy buscando la llave de la habitación - I'm looking for the room key

Necesito cambiar dinero - I need to exchange money

¿Cuál es la moneda local? - What is the local currency?

Aún no sé cuál será mi itinerario - I still don't know what my itinerary will be

Aviación - Aviation

El piloto del avión es hábil - The pilot of the plane is skilled

Mi vuelo sale desde esa puerta de embarque - My flight leaves from that gate

El vuelo proveniente de Cancún está retrasado - The flight from Cancun is delayed

Juan despacha su equipaje - Juan checks in his luggage

La tripulación es amable - The crew is friendly

Trenes - Trains

El tren llega al andén - The train reaches the platform

Vivo cerca de las vías del tren - I live near the train tracks

El tren tiene seis vagones - The train has six carriages

La locomotora va al frente - The train's locomotive is at the front

El maquinista es muy joven - The train driver is very young

Navegación - Navigation

La proa es la parte delantera del barco - The bow is the front of the boat

El crucero es muy lujoso - The cruise is very luxurious

El capitán maneja el timón - The captain handles the wheel

Mi tío compró una lancha - My uncle bought a boat

Los camarotes son pequeños - The cabins are small

Lugares - Places

Voy a la terminal de autobuses - I go to the bus terminal

El aeropuerto está muy lejos - The airport is too far

La estación de tren es muy antigua - The train station is very old

El puerto es grande - The port is big

En el muelle hay gaviotas - There are seagulls on the pier

Alojamiento - Lodging

Me hospedo en un hotel - I am staying in a hotel

Luisa pasa la noche en un hostal - Luisa spends the night in a hostel

Necesito una habitación doble - I need a double room

Hay pocos huéspedes en el hotel - There are few guests in the hotel

Esta cadena hotelera es muy conocida - This hotel chain is well known

El recepcionista es alto - The receptionist is tall

El conserje del hotel es simpático - The hotel concierge is friendly

Fernando se registra en el mostrador del hotel - Fernando checks in at the hotel counter

La cabaña está cerca de la playa - The cabin is close to the beach

El fin de semana voy a ir a un campamento - On the weekend I'm going to camp

Chapter 29 - Prepositions (part II)

A few chapters ago, we started learning prepositions, remember?

You already learned how to use *a, con, de, desde, en, hacia, hasta, sin* and *sobre.* Now, in this chapter, we'll learn the rest of them: *ante, bajo, contra, durante, entre, mediante, para, por, según* and *tras*. These are the slightly harder ones.

Por and *para* are especially difficult for non-natives, since they are both equivalente to *for*. English speakers mix them just as much as Spanish speakers mix *in, on* and *at* (which are all equivalent to *en*).

Let's see the most common translations of these prepositions:

ante is *before, in front of.*

bajo is *under.*

contra is *against.*

durante is *during.*

entre is *between.*

mediante is *through, via.*

para is *for, to.*

por is *for, by.*

según is *according to.*

tras is *behind, after*.

Now, let's practice them with 50 example sentences:

ante - before, in front of

El león se para ante el oso - The lion stands before the bear

María se ríe ante su hermana - María laughs in front of her sister

El ministro cedió ante las presiones - The minister gave in to the pressure

Él es muy fuerte ante las adversidades - He is very strong in the face of adversity

Ante la duda, soy prudente - When in doubt, I am prudent

bajo - under

El perro se esconde bajo la cama - The dog hides under the bed

Lucas nada bajo el agua - Lucas swims in the water

Hace diez grados bajo cero - It's ten degrees below zero

Estamos bajo la sombra del árbol - We are under the shade of the tree

Ellos actúan bajo las directivas del jefe - They act under the directives of the boss

contra - against

La tortuga nada contra la corriente - The turtle swims against the current

Me apoyo contra el árbol - I lean against the tree

El gato se choca contra la pared - The cat crashes into the wall

El equipo rojo se enfrenta contra el azul - The red team faces the blue team

Hay una marcha contra el gobierno - There is a demonstration against the government

durante - during

Los osos hibernan durante el invierno - Bears hibernate during the winter

Estudié abogacía durante muchos años - I studied law for many years

Espero que estés cómodo durante tu estadía - I hope you are comfortable during your stay

Las flores crecen durante el verano - Flowers grow during the summer

Los niños jugaron durante todo el día - The children played all day

entre - between

Hay un jardín entre esos dos edificios - There is a garden between those two buildings

No hay secretos entre ellos - There are no secrets between them

Hay un acuerdo entre los vecinos - There is an agreement between the neighbors

Mis vacaciones son entre enero y marzo - My holidays are between January and March

Ella elige entre el vestido rosa y el negro - She chooses between the pink and the black dress

mediante - through, via

El gobernador lo informó mediante una conferencia de prensa - The governor reported it through a press conference

Mi jefa me paga mediante transferencias bancarias - My boss pays me through bank transfers

La computadora se infectó mediante un virus - The computer got infected by a virus

Norma me saludó mediante un mensaje de texto - Norma greeted me via text message

Se hizo un descubrimiento mediante la observación científica - A discovery was made through scientific observation

para - for, to

Yo compro queso para hacer pizza - I buy cheese to make pizza

Martín se abriga para no pasar frío - Martín bundles up so he doesn't get cold

¿Para qué sirve ese botón? - What is that button for?

Graciela me llama para saludarme - Graciela calls me to say hello

Bárbara toma un taxi para ir al trabajo - Bárbara takes a taxi to go to work

por - for, by

Yo doy un paseo por la playa - I take a walk on the beach

La ley fue promulgada por los congresistas - The law was enacted by the members of the Congress

La miel es fabricada por las abejas - Honey is made by bees

El gato se escapa por la ventana - The cat escapes through the window

Ese árbol ha estado allí por décadas - That tree has been there for decades

según - according to

Según la doctora, estoy muy saludable - According to the doctor, I am very healthy

Según ella, hace calor - According to her, it's hot

Comeremos afuera o adentro, según el clima - We will eat outside or inside depending on the weather

La playa se hace más grande según baja la marea - The beach gets wider as the tide retreats

Según mi intuición, ellos son pareja - According to my intuition, they are a couple

tras - behind, after

Los jugadores corren tras la pelota - Players run after the ball

Mi casa está tras esa montaña - My house is behind that mountain

El suelo quedó brillante tras la limpieza - The floor was shiny after cleaning it

Sebastián fue a su casa tras salir del trabajo - Sebastian went home after leaving work

Mi tío empezó a cantar tras tomar algunas clases - My uncle started singing after taking some lessons

Chapter 30 - Travelling (Part II)

Wow! You made it to the final chapter. *¡Eres genial!*

In this final part, we'll go through 4 useful tips you absolutely need to hear before travelling to a Spanish-speaking country:

1. **Try everything!** Yes, we're talking about food. Well, actually... *don't* try everything. Make sure to be careful with spicy food, especially in countries like Mexico, where things can get pretty hot! Also, make sure you learn about the sanitary conditions of the food and water of the places where you'll be staying if you don't want to end up having your trip ruined due to tummy issues.

2. **Don't plan too much.. nor too little**. It's great to know where you're going, and the specific places you want to know and visit. BUT, if you plan *too much* you might be unpleasantly surprised to find out Latin Americans and Spanish people are laid back, sometimes unpunctual and overall chilled. So, plans might not go the way you thought they would. Try to be flexible. On the other hand, a little planning will be necessary to make the most of your trip, since things like frequency of transportation or accommodation capacity might not be the same everywhere. There are places in Latin America where you can only get to by plane once a week, and don't you dare showing up to Machu Picchu without a ticket!

3. **Make friends!** If you stay with your group of friends or family all day and don't interact with other people, you might miss a great chance to really know the culture of the place you're visiting, the actual awesome places to go to and much more. Meet locals, ask them to show you around or to recommend things to do and experience real Spanish immersion!

4. **Learn Spanish!** Quite obvious, right? And you're already doing it. But we mention it here because you should be aware that Latin America and Spain are not like some northern European countries where everyone speaks English. Depending on the region you visit, you might find little to no English speakers. Also, when you speak the language, you get access to a whole new world: the proper culture of the country. So, before you go, learn spanish and continue practicing during your trip. Try to read signs, leaflets, newspapers, listen to the music, watch movies with locals, buy a Spanish book. You'll come back a true expert!

Now, before we say goodbye, listen to our last short story, that takes place in an airport! We hope we'll see *you* in an airport soon, on the way to the Spanish-speaking world. ¡Adiós!

¿Es él? - Is it him?

Guillermo ajusta su gorra y se pone su nuevo par de gafas negras.

Ese es su uniforme: lo que la gente espera ver de una celebridad en un aeropuerto. Es un disfraz; y uno no muy bueno.

Toma su maleta con rueditas. Después, hace algunos estiramientos y da un par de saltos para entrar en calor.

Es la hora. El recorrido total, entre aduanas, zonas de embarque y cambios de terminal, es de algo así como un kilómetro y medio.

En principio no parece mucho, pero no es fácil hacerlo a toda velocidad.

Guillermo saca el pasaporte de su bolsillo y lo sostiene en la mano, para mayor verosimilitud. Y después, apenas cruza el control migratorio, escucha la primera voz:

—Mira, ¿es él? ¡ES ÉL! —grita alguien.

Una multitud de periodistas se mueve en dirección a él. Rompen el cordón de la policía aeroportuaria. Guillermo corre, pero sabe que los periodistas no son el verdadero problema. Siempre cargan equipos —cámaras, grabadores, micrófonos—, y no están vestidos con ropa apropiada. Usan trajes, tacos. No están listos para correr.

El problema, en realidad, son los fanáticos. Y ellos esperan detrás de la siguiente puerta.

Guillermo toma la ruta planeada: pasa por el *freeshop*, donde escucha muchos gritos, luego corre por la terminal C y, finalmente, llega al estacionamiento. Una multitud de fanáticos con camisetas estampadas y *merchandising* de lo más variado lo persigue.

Pero Guillermo tiene un truco: ni bien cruza la puerta final, se esconde y aprovecha los pocos segundos de ventaja: se quita la gorra, los lentes y el suéter, y los guarda dentro de la maleta, que deja tirada ahí mismo. Cuando sale caminando, nadie en la masa de fanáticos lo mira dos veces.

Una vez terminado su trabajo, busca la furgoneta blanca en la puerta de la terminal A.

Dentro, lo espera otro hombre, el hombre cuyo rostro aparecía en las camisetas estampadas; se parece a Guillermo, aunque no demasiado. Es algo en la forma de la nariz, en el mentón, sobre todo en los labios. Con una gorra y unas buenas gafas, es fácil confundirlos.

—Gracias, Guille —le dice Ricky, la celebridad.

—De nada, jefe —dice Guillermo—. ¿Estuvo todo bien?

—Perfecto. Pasé por la aduana y los controles sin nadie que me molestara. Ahora, vamos a casa.

Vocab:

gorra is cap.

gafas negras is sunglasses.

disfraz is costume.

maleta is luggage.

estiramiento is stretching.

salto is jump.

entrar en calor is to warm up.

recorrido is route.

aduanas is customs.

zona de embarque is boarding area.

periodista is journalist.

camiseta is t-shirt.

furgoneta is van.

nariz is nose.

mentón is chin.

labios is lips.

Now, listen to the story again. And, why not? Go through the entire book one more time, and learn how much *español* you already know.

¡Saludos y mucha suerte!

www.ingramcontent.com/pod-product-compliance
Lightning Source LLC
Chambersburg PA
CBHW081506080526
44589CB00017B/2669